OPPOSING
VIEWPOINTS®
SERIES

School Reform

Other Books of Related Interest:

Opposing Viewpoints Series

Home Schooling

School Vouchers

Teen Drug Abuse

At Issue Series

Do Children Have Rights?

Should Character Be Taught in School?

Should Junk Food Be Sold in Schools?

Current Controversies Series

Teens and Privacy

"Congress shall make
no law ... abridging
the freedom of speech,
or of the press."

First Amendment to the U.S. Constitution

The basic foundation of our democracy is the First Amendment guarantee of freedom of expression. The Opposing Viewpoints Series is dedicated to the concept of this basic freedom and the idea that it is more important to practice it than to enshrine it.

OPPOSING VIEWPOINTS® SERIES

| School Reform

Noah Berlatsky, Book Editor

GREENHAVEN PRESS
A part of Gale, Cengage Learning

GALE
CENGAGE Learning™

Detroit • New York • San Francisco • New Haven, Conn • Waterville, Maine • London

Christine Nasso, *Publisher*
Elizabeth Des Chenes, *Managing Editor*

© 2011 Greenhaven Press, a part of Gale, Cengage Learning.

Gale and Greenhaven Press are registered trademarks used herein under license.

For more information, contact:
Greenhaven Press
27500 Drake Rd.
Farmington Hills, MI 48331-3535
Or you can visit our Internet site at gale.cengage.com

For product information and technology assistance, contact us at

Gale Customer Support, 1-800-877-4253
For permission to use material from this text or product, submit all requests online at
www.cengage.com/permissions

Further permissions questions can be emailed to permissionrequest@cengage.com

Articles in Greenhaven Press anthologies are often edited for length to meet page requirements. In addition, original titles of these works are changed to clearly present the main thesis and to explicitly indicate the author's opinion. Every effort is made to ensure that Greenhaven Press accurately reflects the original intent of the authors. Every effort has been made to trace the owners of copyrighted material.

Cover Image copyright © iStockPhoto.com/lisegagne.

LIBRARY OF CONGRESS CATALOGING-IN-PUBLICATION DATA

School reform / Noah Berlatsky, book editor.
    p. cm. -- (Opposing viewpoints)
    Includes bibliographical references and index.
    ISBN 978-0-7377-4781-2 (hardcover) -- ISBN 978-0-7377-4782-9 (pbk.)
    1. Educational change. 2. Educational evaluation. 3. Educational tests and measurements. I. Berlatsky, Noah.
    LB2806S3424 2010
    379.73--dc22

                                    2010017080

Printed in the United States of America
2 3 4 5 6 7 14 13 12 11 10

Contents

Chapter 1: What Are the Politics of School Reform?

Chapter 2: What Role Should Standardized Tests Play in Evaluating Students?

Chapter 3: What Role Should Testing Play in Evaluating Teachers and Schools?

Chapter 4: What Role Should School Choice Play in School Reform?

Why Consider Opposing Viewpoints?

> *"The only way in which a human being can make some approach to knowing the whole of a subject is by hearing what can be said about it by persons of every variety of opinion and studying all modes in which it can be looked at by every character of mind. No wise man ever acquired his wisdom in any mode but this."*
>
> John Stuart Mill

In our media-intensive culture it is not difficult to find differing opinions. Thousands of newspapers and magazines and dozens of radio and television talk shows resound with differing points of view. The difficulty lies in deciding which opinion to agree with and which "experts" seem the most credible. The more inundated we become with differing opinions and claims, the more essential it is to hone critical reading and thinking skills to evaluate these ideas. Opposing Viewpoints books address this problem directly by presenting stimulating debates that can be used to enhance and teach these skills. The varied opinions contained in each book examine many different aspects of a single issue. While examining these conveniently edited opposing views, readers can develop critical thinking skills such as the ability to compare and contrast authors' credibility, facts, argumentation styles, use of persuasive techniques, and other stylistic tools. In short, the Opposing Viewpoints Series is an ideal way to attain the higher-level thinking and reading skills so essential in a culture of diverse and contradictory opinions.

In addition to providing a tool for critical thinking, Opposing Viewpoints books challenge readers to question their own strongly held opinions and assumptions. Most people form their opinions on the basis of upbringing, peer pressure, and personal, cultural, or professional bias. By reading carefully balanced opposing views, readers must directly confront new ideas as well as the opinions of those with whom they disagree. This is not to argue simplistically that everyone who reads opposing views will—or should—change his or her opinion. Instead, the series enhances readers' understanding of their own views by encouraging confrontation with opposing ideas. Careful examination of others' views can lead to the readers' understanding of the logical inconsistencies in their own opinions, perspective on why they hold an opinion, and the consideration of the possibility that their opinion requires further evaluation.

Evaluating Other Opinions

To ensure that this type of examination occurs, Opposing Viewpoints books present all types of opinions. Prominent spokespeople on different sides of each issue as well as well-known professionals from many disciplines challenge the reader. An additional goal of the series is to provide a forum for other, less known, or even unpopular viewpoints. The opinion of an ordinary person who has had to make the decision to cut off life support from a terminally ill relative, for example, may be just as valuable and provide just as much insight as a medical ethicist's professional opinion. The editors have two additional purposes in including these less known views. One, the editors encourage readers to respect others' opinions—even when not enhanced by professional credibility. It is only by reading or listening to and objectively evaluating others' ideas that one can determine whether they are worthy of consideration. Two, the inclusion of such viewpoints encourages the important critical thinking skill of objectively evaluating an author's credentials and bias. This evaluation will illuminate an author's reasons for taking a particular stance on an issue and will aid in readers' evaluation of the author's ideas.

It is our hope that these books will give readers a deeper understanding of the issues debated and an appreciation of the complexity of even seemingly simple issues when good and honest people disagree. This awareness is particularly important in a democratic society such as ours in which people enter into public debate to determine the common good. Those with whom one disagrees should not be regarded as enemies but rather as people whose views deserve careful examination and may shed light on one's own.

Thomas Jefferson once said that "difference of opinion leads to inquiry, and inquiry to truth." Jefferson, a broadly educated man, argued that "if a nation expects to be ignorant and free ... it expects what never was and never will be." As individuals and as a nation, it is imperative that we consider the opinions of others and examine them with skill and discernment. The Opposing Viewpoints Series is intended to help readers achieve this goal.

David L. Bender and Bruno Leone,
Founders

Introduction

"The failure to ensure that all young people learn what they need to succeed undermines equality and opportunity— the fundamental values of the United States."

—The Bill and Melinda
Gates Foundation

The Bill and Melinda Gates Foundation is the largest transparently operated private foundation in the world, with assets of $33.5 billion dollars as of December 31, 2009, according to its own online fact sheet at www.gatesfoundation .org. One of the Gates Foundation's signature issues has been education, and its huge size and influence has made it a major force in school reform since the early 2000s.

The Gates Foundation has encouraged several different initiatives in school reform. One of their early efforts was a push for smaller schools. The Gates Foundation believed that smaller schools would allow more individual attention to students and therefore increase graduation rates. Jim Shelton, the foundation's program director for education, was quoted by Barbara Miner in a summer 2005 article in *Rethinking Schools* as saying that "'size is an enabler [of learning]. It allows you to have an environment in which kids will know each other and the adults will know the kids.'" Miner added that as of 2005, the foundation had established four hundred small schools and was working to open fifteen hundred more, with about half of those being new schools and half being conversions of larger schools into smaller units.

Unfortunately, the small schools project did not work as well as the Gates Foundation had hoped. *BusinessWeek* reported in a June 26, 2006, cover story that Bill and Melinda

Gates "deserve no better than a C when it comes to improving academic performance," and that the small schools they funded showed little improvement in English and a worsening of math scores. Finally, in a November 11, 2008, speech available online at the Gates Foundation Web site, Bill Gates admitted that despite $2 billion in expenditures, the small schools program had had "disappointing results," which had "showed how hard it can be to convert large, low-performing high schools into smaller, more autonomous schools." Gates concluded that other changes were necessary besides merely changing school size and noted that successful schools had changed curricula, standards, and school hours in addition to altering the size of the schools.

The Gates Foundation has, however, remained "optimistic," and committed to pushing forward school reform. Among other goals, the foundation wants to link teacher pay to student test scores, encourage the development of charter schools that operate separately from the regular public school system, and create common nationwide academic standards. The foundation also wants to improve the use of technology in the classroom. Many of these goals are also shared by the Barack Obama administration, and the Gates Foundation has been working to link its efforts with those of the government in various ways, according to an October 29, 2009, Associated Press article by Libby Quaid and Donna Blankinship. For example, schools that share the goals of the Gates Foundation can receive $250,000 to help them apply for government money from the Obama administration's massive Race to the Top educational program.

Gates argued in a January 25, 2010, article in *Newsweek* that major change in education is necessary. "Our education system has been fundamental to our success as a nation," he said, "but the way we prepare students has barely changed in 100 years. If we don't find ways to improve our schools, making them more effective and more accessible, we won't fulfill our commitment to equal opportunity, and we will become less competitive with other countries."

Not all commentators, however, have been certain that Gates has the right formula for success, or that pushing for rapid change is necessarily the answer. In her 2010 book *The Death and Life of the Great American School System,* education historian Diane Ravitch argues that Gates's focus on charter schools may work no better than his earlier focus on small schools. Ravitch argues that "the strategies now favored by the most powerful forces in the private and public sectors are unlikely to improve American education. Deregulation contributed to the near collapse of our national economy in 2008, and there is no reason to anticipate that it will make education better for our children. . . . Education is too important to relinquish to the vagaries of the market and the good intentions of amateurs."

The viewpoints contained in this book continue this debate over who is best suited to reform schools and how (or even whether) such reform should be done. The chapters ask the questions What Are the Politics of School Reform? What Role Should Standardized Tests Play in Evaluating Students? What Role Should Testing Play in Evaluating Teachers and Schools? and What Role Should School Choice Play in School Reform? Whichever side each author takes in the debate, they all, like Bill and Melinda Gates, believe education is central to how the nation sees itself and what it can achieve.

CHAPTER 1

What Are the Politics of School Reform?

Chapter Preface

School reform often involves a number of explicitly political issues. Some of the most contentious of these have centered on curriculum content. Thus, conservative Christian groups have tried for many years, with varying success, to include the teaching of biblical creationism in schools. On the other hand, many scientists and more liberal groups have argued that evolution should be taught but that creationism should not be.

Biology is not the only area that has been torn by political struggles over the curriculum. For example, history has been a contentious subject for many years. As Mariah Blake noted in the January/February 2010 issue of the *Washington Monthly*, "Up until the 1950s, textbooks painted American history as a steady string of triumphs, but the upheavals of the 1960s shook up old hierarchies, and beginning in the latter part of the decade, textbook publishers scrambled to rewrite their books to make more space for women and minorities." These changes, however, were controversial and were never fully accepted by many conservatives. Thus, Kelly Shackelford writing on the Fox News Web site on March 11, 2010, argued that "a liberal onslaught has been unleashed" to try to change education in Texas. Shackelford accused liberals of trying to cut Christopher Columbus and Thomas Edison out of Texas statewide history standards in order to make way for more diversity and to play down American successes.

The Texas standards have become a nationwide point of contention because Texas has a major influence on the content of textbooks throughout the United States. Jeff Riggenbach in a March 17, 2010, article on the Ludwig von Mises Institute Web site explains, "Texas's importance is directly connected with its size—its population. It's the 2nd most populous state, right after California. It has roughly 25 million residents. . . . Both states set statewide standards for every course offered in their public school systems, then provide copies of these standards to textbook publishers. Who can really blame the publishers if they react by, first, producing textbooks that meet the standards in Texas and California and, then, providing those same textbooks to everybody else in the country, too, whether they like it or not?"

Texas is in general a conservative state, and its board of education is similarly conservative. On March 12, 2010, the board voted to change social studies standards to emphasize the importance of Christianity in America's early years, to give more attention to conservative organizations like the National Rifle Association, and to cut down coverage of founding father Thomas Jefferson, whose ideas about separation of church and state are not popular with many conservatives. "Efforts by Hispanic board members to include more Latino figures as role models for the state's large Hispanic population were consistently defeated," according to James C. McKinley Jr., writing in the *New York Times* on March 12, 2010.

The struggles in Texas about the history curriculum demonstrate one way in which political convictions and goals have fueled school reform. The following viewpoints will examine how politics affects reform in other policy areas.

| "No Child Left Behind is an excellent sword that we can use to open doors for the children we represent."

No Child Left Behind Is a Good Law

Pete Wright

Pete Wright is an attorney who represents children with special educational needs. In the following viewpoint, he argues that the definitions of acceptable reading programs and teacher training in No Child Left Behind (NCLB) are very helpful in protecting special needs students. Wright admits that federal enforcement of NCLB is a problem and that parents often have to bring lawsuits to have the statute implemented. But he concludes that the language of NCLB makes these lawsuits easier to win and can help guarantee better education programs for special needs students.

As you read, consider the following questions:

1. Who is Judy Heumann, and why was she not allowed to attend school in New York City, according to Wright?

2. As cited by the author, what did the National Council on Disability say was a fundamental problem with IDEA?

3. According to Wright, why was the hearing officer on his case relieved that the case was not based on NCLB?

Many people have questions about the No Child Left Behind Act. Some people damn NCLB, some praise it. Others want my opinion about whether the law is good or bad for kids with special educational needs.

No Child Left Behind is a good law. Enforcement of this law (as with enforcement of IDEA)[1] will be a problem.

Some of us old-timers remember the early 1970s, before the special education law was passed. It was perfectly legal for schools to expel children with disabilities permanently for reasons related to their disabilities.

You may know Judy Heumann, former head of special ed for the U.S. Department of Education [USDOE]. Because she was in a wheelchair, she was not allowed to attend school in New York City—she was deemed a "fire hazard."

When Public Law 94-142 (now IDEA) was passed in 1975, schools complained loudly, just as they are complaining about No Child Left Behind today. Initially, several states refused to accept federal special ed funding so they would not have to comply with the law.

During the early 1980s, children with autism in Virginia were deemed to be suffering from a medical condition, and not to have educational disabilities. Decision after decision upheld school districts' right to deny special education services to children with autism.

We've come a long way.

---

1. IDEA (Individuals with Disabilities Education Act) is a federal law regulating how schools treat students with disabilities.

Enforcement Problems

Some people say that if the U.S. Department of Education will not enforce the No Child Left Behind Act, it is a bad law. Enforcement has always been a problem with IDEA. Enforcement will be a problem with No Child Left Behind. This does not make NCLB a bad law.

I think it is unrealistic to expect the U.S. Department of Education to do this. As a practical matter, they view themselves as educators, not as law enforcers or prosecutors. They are different from the investigators and attorneys with the U.S. Department of Justice—and that's a problem.

From the passage of P.L. 94-142 in 1975, move forward 25 years to 2000, when the National Council on Disability published their explosive report, "Back to School on Civil Rights" (also called the IDEA Compliance Report).

On January 25, 2000, the National Council on Disability (NCD) reported to the President and Congress that as "a result of 25 years of nonenforcement by the Federal Government, parents are still a main enforcement vehicle for ensuring compliance with IDEA."

In their report, NCD explained that a fundamental problem with IDEA is that the U.S. Department of Education is a funding and programmatic agency, not an enforcement agency. . . .

NCLB in Special Education Litigation

I am now using language from No Child Left Behind in special ed[ucation] cases.

In a recent due process case, we raised No Child Left Behind issues in correspondence before we requested the hearing.

I wrote a letter to the special education director to request information about their reading program and quoted portions of NCLB as a basis for my request. This letter began to create the theme of the case—that the child did not learn to read because the school district failed to use a research based reading program. I included the definition of scientifically based reading research and the definition of essential components of reading instruction, per the statute, in my letter.

I also raised questions about using an aide who did not meet the minimal qualifications for a paraprofessional under No Child Left Behind. In addition to verbatim quotes from NCLB, I attached copies of the critical NCLB statutes to my letter. . . .

When the parents requested the due process hearing, the school had still not provided the requested information, so I wrote a letter to the school board attorney, with a copy to the Hearing Officer. I included a copy of my earlier letter, quoted a portion of it, and explained that:

"We are waiting for the 'scientifically based research' that was relied upon to support the continued use of 'Patterns for Success' with K [a student].

"Please advise if you are willing to stipulate for the record that the York County School Division:

- "Did not rely on any scientifically based research to support the continued use of 'Patterns for Success' with K, and;

- "That there is no scientifically based research, (as defined in NCLB above), that supports the use of said program with children with dyslexia.

"If you are unwilling to enter into such a stipulation, please advise as to when the requested information will be produced, or, in the alternative, if it will be necessary that I request the Hearing Officer to issue a subpoena *duces tecum* [a command to produce documents] to force production of that information."

This caused a ruckus and led to a telephone conference call with the Hearing Officer.

During the conference call, the Hearing Officer asked if I was asking that he make a finding that the school district's program was in violation of NCLB.

I replied, "Oh no. We are simply arguing that the school district failed to teach this child to read because they used a program that cost about $50, used an untrained aide, and no one involved had the necessary knowledge or skills to teach the child to read. NCLB provides very clear law about reading, reading research, and staff training and qualifications. But I am bringing this case under IDEA, not under NCLB."

The Hearing Officer was relieved. He said he had reviewed information about NCLB. . . . He said it seemed that no one had a good handle on the law, that opinions were all over the place. I agreed that there are many misunderstandings about the law.

He added, "but all children must be taught to read, staff must be well trained, and schools must use reading programs that are research based."

I replied, "Yes sir, and that's the theme of our case." At that point I felt that we had won, although the trial was still three weeks away.

NCLB Opens Doors

During the hearing, I hammered the school district's inadequate efforts to teach the child how to read. We won.

While the Hearing Officer never mentioned NCLB in his ruling, accountability, charting educational progress, and the need to teach reading skills [were] central to his ruling.

This is how I am using No Child Left Behind in special education litigation—I use the definitions of reading, scientifically based reading research, diagnostic reading assessment, and essential components of reading programs from the law, and appropriate training of qualified staff. . . .

No Child Left Behind is an excellent sword that we can use to open doors for the children we represent.

Yes, until the USDOE gives over enforcement authority of IDEA and NCLB, we will have enforcement problems. That is a separate issue, and should not detract from the value of the No Child Left Behind law.

What do I think about the No Child Left Behind law? I think it's great!

| "No Child Left Behind has actually made it harder for states to improve the quality of teaching."

No Child Left Behind Is a Bad Law

Linda Darling-Hammond

Linda Darling-Hammond is the Charles E. Ducommon Professor of Education at Stanford University and the author of The Right to Learn: A Blueprint for Creating Schools That Work. *In the following viewpoint she argues that No Child Left Behind (NCLB) has hurt schools by emphasizing testing rather than focusing on more important funding issues. She adds that the testing and accountability provisions of NCLB have caused a shrinking of the curriculum and have made innovative reforms more difficult. NCLB has particularly hurt poorer students, she argues, by encouraging school districts to push them out of school in an effort to raise test scores.*

As you read, consider the following questions:

1. According to Darling-Hammond, NCLB attempts to raise achievement by setting annual test-score targets based on what long-term goal?

2. How does the United States rank compared with other countries in mathematics, according to the author?

3. What negative educational consequences does Darling-Hammond say occur when NCLB labels a school as failing?

When Congress passed George W. Bush's signature education initiative, No Child Left Behind [(NCLB) in 2002], it was widely hailed as a bipartisan breakthrough—a victory for American children, particularly those traditionally underserved by public schools. Now, five years later [2007], the debate over the law's reauthorization has a decidedly different tone. As the House and Senate consider whether the law should be preserved—and if so, how it should be changed—high-profile Republicans are expressing their disenchantment with NCLB, while many newly elected Democrats are seeking a major overhaul as well.

What happened? Most discussions focus on the details of the more than 1,000-page law, which has provoked widespread criticism for the myriad issues it has raised. All of its flaws deserve scrutiny in the reauthorization debate, but it's also worth taking a step back to ask what the nation actually needs educationally. Lagging far behind our international peers in educational outcomes—and with one of the most unequal educational systems in the industrialized world—we need, I believe, something much more than and much different from what NCLB offers. We badly need a national policy that enables schools to meet the intellectual demands of the twenty-first century. More fundamentally, we need to pay off the educational debt to disadvantaged students that has accrued over centuries of unequal access to quality education.

Promises and Problems

In 2002 civil rights advocates praised NCLB for its emphasis on improving education for students of color, those living in poverty, new English learners and students with disabilities. NCLB aims to raise achievement and close the achievement gap by setting annual test-score targets for subgroups of students, based on a goal of "100 percent proficiency" by 2014. These targets are tied to school sanctions that can lead to school reconstitutions or closures, as well as requirements for student transfers. In addition, NCLB requires schools to hire "highly qualified teachers" and states to develop plans to provide such teachers.

NCLB contains some major breakthroughs. First, by flagging differences in student performance by race and class, it shines a spotlight on longstanding inequalities and could trigger attention to the needs of students neglected in many schools. Second, by insisting that all students are entitled to qualified teachers, the law has stimulated recruitment efforts in states where low-income and "minority" students have experienced a revolving door of inexperienced, untrained teachers. While recent studies have found that teacher quality is a critical influence on student achievement, teachers are the most inequitably distributed school resource. This first-time-ever recognition of students' right to qualified teachers is historically significant.

This noble agenda, however, has been nearly lost in the law's problematic details. Dubbed No Child Left Untested, No School Board Left Standing and No Child's Behind Left, among other nicknames, the law has been protested by more than twenty states and dozens of school districts that have voted to resist specific provisions. One state and a national teachers' association have brought lawsuits against the federal government based on the unfunded costs and dysfunctional side effects of the law. Critics claim that the law's focus on complicated tallies of multiple-choice-test scores has dumbed down the curriculum, fostered a "drill and kill" approach to teaching, mistakenly labeled successful schools as failing, driven teachers and middle-class students out of public schools and harmed special education students and English-language learners through inappropriate assessments and efforts to push out low-scoring students in order to boost scores. Indeed, recent analyses have found that rapid gains in education outcomes stimulated by reforms in the 1990s have stalled under NCLB, with math increases slowing and reading on the decline.

At base, the law has misdefined the problem. It assumes that what schools need is more carrots and sticks rather than fundamental changes.

Funding, Not Testing

Most centrally, the law does not address the profound educational inequalities that plague our nation. With high-spending schools outspending low-spending schools at least three to one in most states, multiplied further by inequalities across states, the United States has the most inequitable education system in the industrialized world. School funding lawsuits brought in more than twenty-five states describe apartheid schools serving low-income students of color with crumbling facilities, overcrowded classrooms, out-of-date textbooks, no science labs, no art or music courses and a revolving door of untrained teachers, while their suburban counterparts, spending twice as much for students with fewer needs, offer expansive libraries, up-to-date labs and technology, small classes, well-qualified teachers and expert specialists, in luxurious facilities.

The funding allocated by NCLB—less than 10 percent of most schools' budgets—does not meet the needs of the under-resourced schools, where many students currently struggle to learn. Nor does the law require that states demonstrate progress toward equitable and adequate funding or greater opportunities to learn. Although NCLB requires "highly qualified teachers," the lack of a federal teacher supply policy makes this a hollow promise in many communities.

At a time when the percentage of Americans living in severe poverty has reached a thirty-two-year high, NCLB seeks to improve the schools poor students attend through threats and sanctions rather than the serious investments in education and welfare such an effort truly requires. As Gloria Ladson-Billings, former president of the American Educational Research Association, has noted, the problem we face is less an "achievement gap" than an educational debt that has accumulated over centuries of denied access to education and employment, reinforced by deepening poverty and resource inequalities in schools. Until American society confronts the accumulated educational debt owed to these students and takes responsibility for the inferior resources they receive, Ladson-Billings argues, children of color and of poverty will continue to be left behind.

Disincentives for Improving Learning

Even if NCLB funding were to increase, its framework does not allow for important structural changes—for example, a system of teacher preparation and professional development that would routinely produce high-quality teaching; curriculums and assessments that encourage critical thinking and performance skills; high-quality preschool education, libraries and learning materials; and healthcare for poor children. Instead, the law wastes scarce resources on a complicated test score game that appears to be narrowing the curriculum, uprooting successful programs and pushing low-achieving students out of many schools.

To go back to first principles, we must ask what US schools should be doing in a world where education is increasingly essential and the nature of knowledge is rapidly changing. What would we need to do to graduate all of our students with the ability to apply knowledge to complex problems, communicate and collaborate effectively and find and manage information?

We might want to be doing some of the things that higher-achieving countries have been doing over the past twenty years as they have left us further and further behind educationally. As an indicator of the growing distance, the United States ranks twenty-eighth of forty countries in mathematics, right above Latvia, and graduates only about 75 percent of students, instead of the more than 95 percent now common elsewhere. Most high-achieving countries not only provide high-quality universal preschool and healthcare for children; they also fund their schools centrally and equally, with additional funds going to the neediest schools. Furthermore, they support a better-prepared teaching force—funding competitive salaries and high-quality teacher education, mentoring and ongoing professional development for all teachers. NCLB's answer to the problem of preparing teachers for the increasingly challenging job they face has been to call for alternative routes that often reduce training for the teachers of the poor.

Finally, high-achieving nations focus their curriculums on critical thinking and problem solving, using exams that require students to conduct research and scientific investigations, solve complex real-world problems and defend their ideas orally and in writing. These assessments are not used to rank or punish schools, or to deny promotion or diplomas to students. (In fact, several countries have explicit proscriptions against such practices.) They are used to evaluate curriculum and guide investments in learning—in short, to help schools improve. Finally, by asking students to show what they know through real-world applications of knowledge, these other nations' assessment systems encourage serious intellectual activities that are being driven out of many US schools by the tests promoted by NCLB.

Narrowing the Curriculum

No Child Left Behind has actually made it harder for states to improve the quality of teaching. At the core of these problems is an accountability system borrowed from Texas and adminis-

Impossible Goals

The goal set by Congress [in No Child Left Behind] of 100 percent proficiency [for all children in reading and math] by 2014 is an aspiration; it is akin to a declaration of belief. Yes, we do believe that all children can learn and should learn. But as a goal, it is utterly out of reach. No one truly expects that all students will be proficient by the year 2014, although NCLB's most fervent supporters often claimed that it was feasible. Such a goal has never been reached by any state or nation. In their book about NCLB, [Chester] Finn and [Frederick] Hess acknowledge that no educator believes this goal is attainable; they write, "Only politicians promise such things." . . . But if all students are not on track to be proficient by 2014, then schools will be closed, teachers will be fired, principals will lose their jobs, and some—perhaps many—public schools will be privatized. All because they were not able to achieve the impossible.

The consequence of mandating an unattainable goal, Finn and Hess say, is to undermine states that have been doing a reasonably good job of improving their schools and to produce "a compliance-driven regimen that recreates the very pathologies it was intended to solve."

Diane Ravitch,
The Death and Life of the Great American School System,
2010.

tered by an Education Department with a narrow view of what constitutes learning. This system requires testing every student in math, reading and, soon, science and issuing sanctions to schools that do not show sufficient progress for each subpopulation of students toward an abstract goal of "100 percent proficiency" on state tests—with benchmarks that vary from state to state.

Ironically, states that set high standards risk having the most schools labeled "failing" under NCLB. Thus Minnesota, where eighth graders are first in the nation in mathematics and on a par with the top countries in the world, had 80 percent of schools on track to be labeled failing according to the federal rules. In addition, states that earlier created forward-looking performance assessment systems like those used abroad have begun to abandon them for antiquated, machine-scored tests that more easily satisfy the law. As emphasis on drilling for multiple-choice tests has increased, the amount of research, project work and scientific inquiry has declined, and twelfth grade reading scores have dropped nationwide.

The Education Department has discouraged states from using more instructionally useful forms of assessment that involve teachers in scoring tasks requiring extensive writing and analysis. Connecticut, Maine, Rhode Island, Nebraska and Vermont, among others, had to wrestle with the department to maintain their sophisticated performance-based assessment systems, which resemble those used in high-scoring nations around the world. Connecticut, which assesses students with open-ended tasks like designing, conducting and analyzing a science experiment (and not coincidentally ranks first in the nation in academic performance), sued the federal government for the funds needed to maintain its assessments on an "every child, every year" basis. The Education Secretary suggested the state drop these tasks for multiple-choice tests. Thus the administration of the law is driving the US curriculum in the opposite direction from what a twenty-first–century economy requires.

Preventing Reform

Other dysfunctional consequences derive from the law's complicated accountability scheme, which analysts project will label between 85 and 99 percent of the nation's public schools "failing" within the next few years, even when they are high-performing, improving in achievement and closing the gap. This will happen as states raise their proficiency levels to a national benchmark set far above grade level, and as schools must hit targets for test scores and participation rates for each racial/ethnic, language, income and disability group on several tests—often more than thirty in all. Missing any one of these—for example, having 94 percent of low-income students take the test instead of 95 percent—causes the school to fail to "make AYP" (adequate yearly progress).

Worse still, there is a Catch-22 [a problem with no go solution] for those serving English-language learners and special-needs students. In *Alice in Wonderland* fashion, the law assigns these students to special subgroups because they do not meet the proficiency standard, and they are removed from the subgroup as they catch up, so it is impossible for the subgroups ever to be 100 percent proficient. Schools serving a significant share of these learners will inevitably be labeled failing, even if all their students consistently make strong learning gains. Those who warned that the law was a conservative scheme to undermine public schools and establish vouchers were reinforced in their view when the Bush administration's recent reauthorization plan recommended that students in schools that do not achieve their annual test benchmarks be offered vouchers at public expense.

As a result of these tortuous rules, more than 40 percent of the nation's public schools have been placed on intervention status at some point in the past four years, including some of the highest-achieving schools in the nation and many that are narrowing the achievement gap. These schools have sometimes been forced to dismantle successful programs in favor of dubious interventions pushed by the Education Department—including specific reading programs under the Reading First plan, which, the inspector general found, was managed in such a way as to line the pockets of favored publishers while forcing districts to abandon other, more successful reading programs. Although some of these schools are truly failing and require major help to improve, it is impossible to separate them from schools caught in the statistical mousetrap.

Hurting the Poor

At least some of the schools identified as "needing improvement" are surely dismal places where little learning occurs, or are complacent schools that have not attended to the needs of their less advantaged students. It is fair to suggest that students in such schools deserve other choices if the schools cannot change. However, there is growing evidence that the law's strategy for improving schools may, paradoxically, reduce access to education for the most vulnerable students.

NCLB's practice of labeling schools as failures makes it even harder for them to attract and keep qualified teachers. As one Florida principal asked, "Is anybody going to want to dedicate their life to a school that has already been labeled a failure?" What's more, schools that have been identified as not meeting AYP standards must use their federal funds to support choice and "supplemental services," such as privately provided after-school tutoring, leaving them with even fewer resources for their core educational programs. Unfortunately, many of the private supplemental service providers have proved ineffective and unaccountable, and transfers to better schools have been impossible in communities where such schools are unavailable or uninterested in serving students with low achievement, poor attendance and other problems that might bring their own average test scores down. Thus, rather than expanding educational opportunities for low-income students and students of color, the law in many communities further reduces the quality of education available in the schools they must attend.

Perhaps the most adverse unintended consequence of NCLB is that it creates incentives for schools to rid themselves of students who are not doing well, producing higher scores at the expense of vulnerable students' education. Studies have found that sanctioning schools based on average student scores leads schools to retain students in grade so that grade-level scores will look better (although these students ultimately do less well and drop out at higher rates), exclude low-scoring students from admissions and encourage such students to transfer or drop out.

Recent studies in Massachusetts, New York and Texas show how schools have raised test scores while "losing" large numbers of low-scoring students. In a large Texas city, for example, scores soared while tens of thousands of students—mostly African-American and Latino—disappeared from school. Educators reported that exclusionary policies were used to hold back, suspend, expel or counsel out students in order to boost test scores. Overall, fewer than 40 percent of African-American and Latino students graduated. Paradoxically, NCLB's requirement for disaggregating data by race creates incentives for eliminating those at the bottom of each subgroup, especially where schools have little capacity to improve the quality of services such students receive. As a consequence of high-stakes testing, graduation rates for African-American and Latino students have declined in a number of states. In the NCLB paradigm, there is no solution to this problem, as two-way accountability does not exist: The child and the school are accountable to the state for test performance, but the state is not held accountable to the child or his school for providing adequate educational resources.

| "*The Race to the Top is the equivalent of education reform's moon shot.*"

The Race to the Top Program Will Transform Education

Arne Duncan

Arne Duncan is the United States secretary of education. In the following viewpoint, he discusses the Barack Obama Administration's new Race to the Top program, which Duncan says will channel unprecedented amounts of money to education. Duncan argues that the funds, which will be distributed through competitive grants, will help to improve academic standards, collect data, identify and hire effective teachers, and turn around low-performing schools.

As you read, consider the following questions:

1. How does the money allocated for Race to the Top compare to the money allocated for school reform by previous education departments, according to Duncan?

2. How are the four assurances of Race to the Top interrelated, in the author's opinion?

Arne Duncan, "The Race to the Top Begins—Remarks by Secretary Arne Duncan," July 24, 2009, U.S. Department of Education Web site, July 24, 2009. Reproduced by permission.

3. Besides Race to the Top, what other programs for providing funds to schools does Duncan discuss?

For most of its existence, the department [of education] has only had modest discretionary funds available for reform and innovation—and a limited ability to push for better outcomes.

That's about to change. The $4.35 billion dollar Race to the Top program ... is a once-in-a-lifetime opportunity for the federal government to create incentives for far-reaching improvement in our nation's schools.

More Resources than Ever

Since the education department was created in 1980, eight of my predecessors have stood here. They fought to improve our schools, too. But none of them had the resources to encourage innovation that we have today.

In fact, if you take all of the discretionary money for reform that every one of my predecessors had—and then add it all together for the last 29 years in a row—it's still a much smaller money pot for reform than the $4.35 billion Race to the Top fund. . . .

For states, for district leaders, for unions, for business, and for non-profits, the Race to the Top is the equivalent of education reform's moon shot. And the administration is determined—I am determined—not to miss this opportunity.

What is the administration going to be looking for in the Race to the Top competition? We are going to be scrutinizing state applications for a coordinated and deep-seated commitment to reform. And we are going to be awarding grants on a competitive basis in two rounds, allowing first-round losers to make necessary changes and reapply.

We take our cue here from the president. He starts with the understanding that maintaining the status quo in our schools is unacceptable. He recognizes that America needs urgently to reduce its high dropout rates and elevate the quality of K–12 schooling—not just to propel the economic recovery but also because students need stronger skills to compete with students in India and China.

Today, more than ever, better schooling provides a down payment on the nation's future. As President Obama puts it, "education is no longer just a pathway to opportunity and success—it's a prerequisite for success." Yet I think we all know that far too many schools fail to prepare their students today for success in college or a career.

Four Assurances

Under the Race to the Top guidelines, states seeking funds will be pressed to implement four core, interconnected reforms. We sometimes call them the four assurances, and those assurances are what we are going to be looking for from states, districts, and their local partners in reform.

For starters, we expect that winners of the Race to the Top grants will work to reverse the pervasive dumbing down of academic standards and assessments that has taken place in many states.

A low-income, middle school student in San Antonio should not be held to a lower standard in algebra than a middle school student in Shaker Heights [Ohio, an upper-class Cleveland suburb known for its good schools]—or Shanghai [China]. That's why we are looking for Race to the Top states to adopt common, internationally-benchmarked K–12 standards that truly prepare students for college and careers. To speed this process, the Race to the Top program is going to set aside $350 million to competitively fund the development of rigorous, common state assessments.

Second, we want to close the data gap that now handcuffs districts from tracking growth in student learning and improving classroom instruction. Award-winning states will be able to monitor growth in student learning—and identify effective instructional practices.

Third, it is no secret that when it comes to schools, talent matters—tremendously. To boost the quality of teachers and principals, especially in high-poverty schools and hard-to-staff subjects, states and districts should be able to identify effective teachers and principals. At the local level we want to see better strategies in place to reward and retain more top-notch teachers—and improve or replace ones who aren't up to the job.

And finally, to turn around the lowest-performing schools, states and districts must be ready to institute far-reaching reforms, replace school staff, and change the school culture. We cannot continue to tinker in terrible schools where students fall further and further behind, year after year.

Now those are our four assurances, the four core reforms that we are looking for. But I want to be clear that these four reforms are interrelated, so that one reform reinforces the others.

When teachers get better data on student growth, it empowers teachers to tailor classroom instruction to the needs of their students and boost student achievement.

When principals are able to identify their most effective and least effective teachers, it makes it easier for them to place teachers where they are needed most—and provide struggling teachers with help.

When superintendents have the authority to tackle their lowest performing schools by replacing staff and shaking up the school culture, they will have the ability—for the first time—to close or remake the dropout factories in our urban districts that are at the root of our dropout problem.

And when state lawmakers and chief school officers can evaluate the college-readiness of students and their ability to compete with their peers—not just in nearby states but in other nations—state officials will be able to diagnose the strengths and weaknesses of the state system in a global economy—again, for the first time.

Partnership and Competition

The Race to the Top program is going to mark a new federal partnership in education reform with states, districts, and unions to accelerate reform. We are going to be consulting and soliciting the input of all stakeholders, and I plan to hold a conference call for governors, chief state officers, state lawmakers and state school boards.

But I want to be clear that the Race to the Top is also a reform competition, one where states can increase or decrease their odds of winning federal support.

States, for example, that limit alternative routes to certification for teachers and principals, or cap the number of charter schools[1], will be at a competitive disadvantage. And states that explicitly prohibit linking data on achievement or student growth to principal and teacher evaluations will be ineligible for reform dollars until they change their laws.

As big as the Race to the Top fund is, it's not the only major lever for transformational reform. We are also going to be releasing shortly the guidelines for the $3.5 billion Title I School Improvement Grants. And most of that money is going to go to low-income districts that are willing to turn around their lowest-performing schools.

[We will soon] publish the metrics for the competitive $650 million dollar Invest in Innovation Fund, which will award districts and non-profits that are developing cutting-edge reforms, piloting promising new programs or taking proven programs to scale.

We also have $650 million dollars to award in education technology grants to states and districts that are doing a good

---

1. Charter schools receive public money but have different programs and accountability than most public schools. Students generally apply for or choose to attend charter schools.

Obama and Teachers' Unions

The $4.35 billion Race to the Top (RTT) fund lets states apply for grants that focus on a short list of reforms guaranteed to anger one of the Democratic Party's core constituencies, the teachers' unions.... The [Democratic Barack] Obama Administration is about to square off with the unions over perhaps the most controversial classroom issue of all: the idea that teachers should be held accountable for the success or failure of their students.

Gilbert Cruz, Time,
September 14, 2009.

job of using technology to enhance learning. We have $200 million in Recovery Act funding for the Teacher Incentive Fund, which supports performance-based teacher and principal compensation systems in high-need schools. And finally, we have more than $300 million available to help states build data systems that will drive reforms.

I know I've just thrown a lot of numbers and programs at you. But the long and short of it, is that when you add it all up, the department will be disbursing almost $10 billion for education reform.

Ten billion dollars is not chump change. And to every governor who ever aspired to be his state's "education governor," I say: do not let this unprecedented opportunity slip away.

Change Is Possible

Let me close by saying that the president and I are not naïve about the difficulty of reform. I served as superintendent of the Chicago Public Schools for seven years. And I saw first-hand that the system often serves the interests of adults better than its students.

But I don't accept much of the pessimism and age-old apathy about the potential of school reform. During my seven years as CEO of Chicago's schools, tests scores increased on state and national exams, and the percentage of students graduating increased. That happened not just because of the district's efforts but because teachers, community leaders, and parents worked hard to make reform a reality.

Since being confirmed as Secretary, I have visited 23 states and met countless students, teachers, parents and administrators. They are hungering for change. I've seen districts and high-performing schools that are closing achievement gaps, raising graduation rates, and sending disadvantaged young people to college with scholarships in hand.

Since President Obama took office, many states have adopted reforms that would have been almost unthinkable a year ago. [In spring 2009], 46 states signed on to a state-led process to develop a common core of K–12 state standards in English language arts and math. At the same time, states such as Tennessee, Rhode Island, Indiana, Connecticut, Massachusetts, Colorado, and Illinois have lifted restrictions on charter school growth.

So, despite the obstacles, I remain optimistic about America's capacity for transformational change. The edifice of education reform will take years to build. But the Race to the Top starts today.

"*[Race to the Top] will fail if it is merely a one-off trade of cash for this or that new law.*"

The Race to the Top Program Will Probably Fail

Wall Street Journal

The Wall Street Journal *is an international daily newspaper focusing on business news. In the following viewpoint, the paper argues that President Barack Obama's Race to the Top education initiative, which spends billions on education, may not be effective. The paper says that money does not solve educational problems. In addition, though the administration claims that Race to the Top will support and encourage charters, vouchers, and school choice reforms, those efforts may well be blocked by unions. The* Journal *concludes that, in the tradition of education reforms of the past, Race to the Top will probably be mostly ineffectual.*

As you read, consider the following questions:

1. According to the *Journal*, by how much did education funding grow under President George W. Bush?

2. Between 1970 and 2004, how much did education spending rise and how did this compare to increases on national standardized tests, according to the author?

3. What groups does the *Journal* say are opposed to school choice?

The [Barack] Obama Administration unveiled its new "Race to the Top" initiative late last week [July 2009] in which it will use the lure of $4.35 billion in federal cash to induce states to improve their K–12 schools. This is going to be interesting to watch, because if nothing else the public school establishment is no longer going to be able to say that lack of money is its big problem.

More Money May Not Help

Four billion dollars is a lot of money, but it's a tiny percentage of what the U.S. spends on education. The Department of Education estimates that the U.S. as a whole spent $667 billion on K–12 education in the 2008–09 school year alone, up from $553 billion in 2006–07. The [economic] stimulus bill from earlier this year includes some $100 billion more in federal education spending—an unprecedented amount. The tragedy is that nearly all of this $100 billion is being dispensed to the states by formula, which allows school districts to continue resisting reform while risking very little in overall federal funding.

All of this is on top of the education spending boom during the [George W.] Bush years to pay for the 2001 No Child Left Behind [(NCLB) school reform] law. Democrats liked to claim that law was "underfunded," but the reality is that inflation-adjusted Education Department elementary and secondary spending under President Bush grew to $37.9 billion from $28.3 billion, or 34%. NCLB-specific funding rose by more than 40% between 2001 and 2008.

It's also worth noting that the U.S. has been trying without much success to spend its way to education excellence for decades. Between 1970 and 2004, per-pupil outlays more than doubled in real terms, and the federal portion of that spending nearly tripled. Yet reading scores on national standardized tests have remained relatively flat. Black and Hispanic students are doing better, but they continue to lag far behind white students in both test scores and graduation rates.

More Choice Is Needed

So now comes "Race to the Top," which the Obama Administration claims will reward only those states that raise their academic standards, improve teacher quality and expand the reach of charter schools.[1] "This competition will not be based on politics, ideology or the preferences of a particular interest group," said President Obama. "Instead, it will be based on a simple principle—whether a state is ready to do what works. We will use the best data available to determine whether a state can meet a few key benchmarks for reform, and states that outperform the rest will be rewarded with a grant."

Sounds great, though this White House is, at the behest of the unions, also shuttering a popular school voucher[2] program that its own evaluation shows is improving test scores for low-income minorities in Washington, D.C. The Administration can expect more such opposition to "Race to the Top." School choice is anathema to the nation's two largest teachers unions, the National Education Association [NEA] and the American Federation of Teachers, which also oppose paying teachers for performance rather than for seniority and credentials.

1. Charter schools receive public money, but have different programs and accountability than most public schools. Students generally apply for or choose to attend charter schools.
2. School tuition vouchers are certificates issued by the government, which parents can use to pay for a private school for their children.

NEA President Dennis Van Roekel told the *Washington Post* that charter schools and merit pay raise difficult issues for his members, yet Education Secretary Arne Duncan has said states that block these reforms could jeopardize their grant eligibility. We'll see who blinks first. The acid test is whether Messrs. Duncan and Obama are willing to withhold money from politically important states as the calendar marches toward 2012 [a presidential election year].

Race to the Top is bound to have some impact, and lawmakers in several states—including Tennessee, Rhode Island, Louisiana and Massachusetts—already have passed charter-friendly legislation in hopes of tapping the fund. But the exercise will fail if it is merely a one-off trade of cash for this or that new law. The key is whether the money can be used to promote enough school choice and other reforms that induce school districts to change how the other $800 billion or so is spent.

Charter schools and voucher programs regularly produce better educational outcomes with less money. But as long as most education spending goes to support the status quo, Race to the Top will be mostly a case of political show and tell.

> "Over-reliance on local property taxes significantly underfunds schools in many property-poor communities."

Illinois School Funding Must Be More Equitable to Help Poorer Schools

Center for Tax and Budget Accountability

The Center for Tax and Budget Accountability (CTBA) is an Illinois nonprofit, bipartisan research and advocacy think tank committed to justice in tax, spending, and economic policies. In the following viewpoint, CTBA argues that the reliance on local property taxes to fund schools in Illinois results in differences in funding between the wealthiest school districts and the rest of the districts. Because of these funding differences, students in poorer districts have less success than children in wealthier districts, according to CTBA. CTBA concludes that Illinois' funding structure does not deliver a good education to children in poorer districts, especially downstate students and those in African American and Hispanic communities.

"Chapters: I, II, III and VI," *Money Matters: How the Illinois School Funding System Creates Significant Educational Inequities That Impact Most Students in the State*, September 2008. Copyright © 2008 Center for Tax and Budget Accountability. Reproduced by permission.

As you read, consider the following questions:

1. What is the difference between Foundation Formula districts and Alternative Formula or Flat Grant districts, in the author's opinion?

2. According to CTBA, academic performance on state tests increases when there is an increase of how much in instructional expenditure per student?

3. What percentage of Illinois students attend Flat Grant or Alternative Formula districts and what percent attend Foundation Formula districts, according to the author?

No single policy issue in Illinois has generated more controversy—and less action—than school funding reform. For well over three decades, various attempts at education funding reform have been brought forth, only to generate heated debate and intense media coverage, but not much in the way of meaningful reforms. By now, most are familiar with the basic complaint—Illinois fails to fund education adequately from state-based revenue, ranking 49th out of 50 states in the portion of education funded by state money. This in turn pushes the primary obligation for education funding down to local resources, primarily property taxes, creating great disparities between districts across Illinois, based on local property wealth.

Over-Reliance on Local Taxes

Proponents of reform have argued that this over-reliance on local property taxes significantly underfunds schools in many property-poor communities, resulting in the children who live in those areas receiving an inadequate education. Opponents respond that education has all the resources it needs, and additional investment will not generate better academic outcomes. The sheer complexity of the state's education funding regimen makes it difficult for citizens and policymakers alike to determine which arguments have substance.

To date, much of the conversation has focused on funding and quality differentials between the wealthiest school districts and the most impoverished. Certainly, the contrasts there are striking. The untold story, however, is even more compelling. It focuses not just on the very top versus the very bottom, but rather the differentials between the wealthiest school districts in Illinois—versus the vast majority of districts that provide public education to over three-quarters of the children in our state. The data here are stark and telling, revealing meaningful differences in school funding, teacher quality and academic performance that are truly statewide.

Moreover, substantive differentials in the aforesaid categories exist when affluent districts, which are concentrated north of Interstate 80, are compared to downstate school districts. Racial inequities also emerge as a significant problem in Illinois, with African American and Hispanic children far more likely to attend schools in high poverty areas, with fewer resources, less qualified teachers and lower academic outcomes than their white peers. . . .

How Illinois Schools Are Funded

Like most states, Illinois has adopted a "foundation level" approach to funding K–12 education. Under this approach, the General Assembly [the state legislature] each year determines a minimum amount of basic education funding per student that should be available to all schools, literally, the "Foundation Level." It is important to understand that the per-student Foundation Level does not equate to an amount that is sufficient to cover all the costs of education. In fact, the Foundation Level is primarily intended to cover instructional costs like academic programs and teacher salaries, and specifically does not account for such necessary expenses as transportation and special education. The Foundation Level also does not include any adjustments for poverty. Instead, much as the

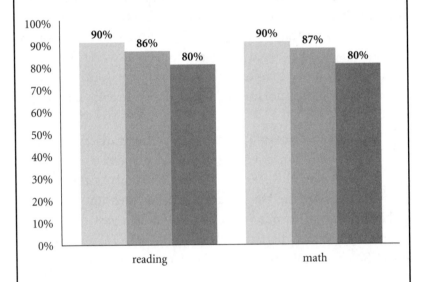

Percentage of Students Meeting or Exceeding ISAT Standards (Grade 8, 2006)

The ISAT is the Illinois State Achievement Test, Flat Grant districts are the wealthiest school districts; Foundation Formula districts are the poorest school districts.

Flat Grant

Alternative Formula

Foundation Formula

TAKEN FROM: CTBA, *Money Matters: How the Illinois School Funding System Creates Educational Inequities that Impact Most Students in the State,* September 2008, p. 10.

name itself implies, the Foundation Level is the basic building block of school funding, upon which other education funding items are layered.

Once the Foundation Level is set for a school year, the Illinois State Board of Education (ISBE) separates school districts into the following three funding categories, based on their local property wealth: (i) "Flat Grant" districts, which have the greatest amount of available local property wealth;

(ii) "Alternative Formula" districts, which have the second greatest amount of available property wealth; and (iii) "Foundation Formula" districts, which include most school districts, and which have available local property wealth that ranges from very low to just above average. Next, ISBE applies a different funding formula to each type of district, to determine how much (if any) of the Foundation Level per student the state will pay in that district, and how much of the Foundation Level will be covered by local property tax revenues. Note that, in each case, the formula assumes that local resources will cover at least a portion of the basic, Foundation Level per student.

Foundation Formula districts are those districts which ISBE determines can cover less than 93 percent of the Foundation Level per child as set by the General Assembly in a given year. Under the base Foundation Formula, the state then makes up the difference (in most cases). The vast majority of Illinois' 870 school districts—81 percent—receive general state aid (GSA) for basic education from the state under this formula. Over 1,600,000 students, or roughly 77 percent of the state's K–12 student body population, attend Foundation Level districts.

The remaining school districts have so much local property wealth that they can cover more than 93 percent of the Foundation Level of support per student with local property tax revenue. Depending on how much more of the Foundation Level a wealthier district can cover, it gets categorized as either "Alternative Formula" or "Flat Grant" by ISBE. It will still receive some GSA from the state, but not [an amount equal to the] full Foundation Formula.

Alternative Formula districts are those districts ISBE determines have the ability to cover between 93 percent and 175 percent of the current year's Foundation Level. Under the Alternative Formula, districts receive GSA from the state ranging from about five percent to seven percent of the then current

Foundation Level. About 18 percent of the students in Illinois attend Alternative Formula districts, which overall account for 15 percent of all 870 school districts.

Flat Grant districts have the most local property wealth of all school districts. Under the state's school funding formula, these districts cover 175 percent or more of the then current Foundation Level per student with local property tax revenue. Instead of receiving any formula-based GSA for education, these districts receive a flat grant of $218 per student from the state. Just under five percent of the 870 school districts in Illinois are Flat Grant districts, which in 2007–2008 were attended by 94,885 students, or roughly four and one-half percent (4.5%) of the state's K–12 student body.

Main Findings

- There are significant differences in key metrics such as teacher quality and student performance, between the wealthier Flat Grant and Alternative Formula districts on the one hand, and the Foundation Formula districts which the vast majority of Illinois students attend on the other.

- Significant funding and educational differences also emerge when affluent, Flat Grant districts are compared to "downstate" school districts, defined as school districts located south of Interstate 80.

- The significant qualitative and outcome differences between wealthier Flat Grant and Alternative Formula districts on the one hand, and Foundation Formula districts on the other, is strongly related to both available local resources and instructional expenditures per student.

- There is a strong correlation between increasing instructional expenditures per student by anywhere from $1,000–$2,200, and academic performance, as measured by the Illinois State Achievement Test.

- This strong correlation between increased instructional expenditures and improved academic performance is evident in both school districts with low poverty (3%–8% low income rates) and significant poverty (27%–32% low income rates).

- Minorities, particularly African Americans and Hispanics, are significantly over-represented in schools with high poverty rates, with over 93 percent of all African American children and over 66 percent of all Hispanic children attending school districts with low income rates of 30 percent or greater.

- Disparities in both quality of teachers and academic performance between primarily Caucasian and primarily minority school districts in Illinois are material, and correlate to instructional expense per child, local property wealth, and inadequate state funding.

- The $2,324 difference in average instructional expense per student between wealthy Flat Grant districts that only 4.5 percent of K–12 students attend, and the Foundation Formula districts that 77 percent of all K–12 students attend, is greater than the $1,003 average per child instructional expense difference between the lowest and highest poverty school districts in Illinois.

- The greatest differential of $2,421 in average instructional expense per student exists between Flat Grant districts and downstate districts (located south of Interstate 80).

Illinois Schools Are Unequal

The 23 percent of Illinois students fortunate enough to attend school in wealthy Flat Grant and Alternative Formula districts, receive a better education, with higher quality teachers and significantly more spent on instruction, that do the vast majority of Illinois students—the 77 percent who attend Foundation Formula districts. In turn, those same children attending Flat Grant and Alternative Formula schools out-perform their peers academically, and at least some of that enhanced academic performance correlates to enhanced funding. These educational differentials affect the entire state of Illinois, and have been particularly harsh for students of color—African Americans and Hispanics.

This inequality is not caused by any misdeeds of Flat Grant and Alternative Formula districts. Far from it. In fact, Flat Grant and Alternative Formula communities have stepped to the plate to fund a quality education. This leaves most students in Illinois, particularly low and middle income children, children of color, and children who live downstate, to attend schools reliant on state-based funding, which simply has not been sufficient to deliver a quality education, whether measured by instructional expense per child, the EFAB [Education Funding Advisory Board] Foundation Level standard, teacher quality or the all important academic performance.

| "Taxpayers deserve relief from ... taxes and spending. Illinois school children deserve a better education."

Deep Tax Cuts and Less Spending Would Improve All Illinois Schools

Bruno Behrend

Bruno Behrend is a lawyer, entrepreneur, and host of the Extreme Wisdom *radio program in Waukegan, Illinois. In the following viewpoint, he argues that Illinois should dramatically lower property taxes, which currently fund schools, and shift the funding burden instead to state taxes. Centralized funds will make change easier, he contends. In addition, Behrend maintains, school districts should be eliminated; instead, all schools should be changed into charter schools, and all students should receive vouchers that can be used at any school. Behrend argues that his reforms would cause radical improvement in schools and deep cuts in taxes.*

As you read, consider the following questions:

1. According to Behrend, where does Illinois rank in school spending?

Bruno Behrend, "Executive Summary of a Plan for a Fundamental Reform of Illinois' Tax and Education Systems," ExtremeWisdom.com. Reproduced by permission.

2. What tax increases are proposed by HB 750, according to the author?

3. How does Behrend propose to eliminate the problem of "teaching to the test?"

Before the 2006 elections, Illinois Governor Rod Blagojevich [a Democrat] announced a grand new scheme to "fund education" with yet another application of Illinois Lottery money. In this scheme, the lottery was to be "privatized," with the proceeds to be used for funding schools. His opponent, [Republican] Judy Baar Topinka, ran on a platform of giving [Chicago] Mayor [Richard] Daley his coveted Chicago Casino.

These are more examples of the lack of seriousness on the part of Illinois' political class. Illinois elected officials are basically playing shell games with state revenue streams while ignoring the state's looming financial debacle. Something must be done to break the tax-and-spend cycle that plagues Illinois. This [viewpoint] summarizes a real plan for reform. Unlike the Governor's and the legislature's shell games and Band-Aids, it actually solves specific problems. Let's start by defining what those problems are.

No Tax Increases

State of Illinois would be considered legally bankrupt if it were held to the standards of the private sector, and even [the standards of] some states. Most legislators believe we can tax or grow our way out of the problem. We can't. Tax increases will only provide incentives for more individuals and businesses to leave Illinois. Though politically difficult, combining spending cuts with a change in Illinois tax structure is a superior solution. The question is, "Where is it possible to cut?"

The answer is to curtail the massive spending increases in the state's broken and unsustainable education bureaucracy. If we make the transition to a smaller and more effective education system, we can create dynamic benefits for Illinois children and taxpayers.

The Fundamental Reform Plan summarized in this [viewpoint] details the numerous benefits of dramatic reform, the most important of which include;

- *A large phased-in tax cut for most Illinois citizens and businesses*

- *Equalized funding for Illinois' school children*

- *A dramatic increase in local control of schools*

- *A dynamic education system that is there for the citizens—not politically powerful interests*

- *Increased revenues for the state government.*

It would be an understatement to say that this proposal represents a bold, maybe even radical, blueprint for reforming Illinois. Frankly, the vast majority of people familiar with Illinois politics will feel compelled to say something like "Interesting idea, but it's politically impossible."

Though we understand such a reaction, we ask you to keep an open mind. *The moment one takes the position good ideas are "impossible," they unwittingly rubberstamp the status quo.* It is our view that the status quo in Illinois politics is unacceptable. With that in mind, let's begin with the main features of this proposal.

Reform Proposals

Tax Reform

- Completely Repeals/Phases-Out of the Local Property Tax for Education

- Increases State Taxes . . .

Education Reform

- Uses existing and increased state revenues to *equally fund every child in Illinois* with a Scholarship (between $6,500–7,500 indexed for inflation) redeemable at any accredited school

- Phases out the "school district" as a governmental entity

- Converts every public school in Illinois into an independent "Charter School"[1]

- Replaces State Education Mandates with a system of annual, uniform, content-specific tests that show progress.

Impact of Reforms

As noted before, these reforms are dramatic, but they are dramatically positive for most of Illinois. These positive benefits include;

- Substantial relief for Illinois taxpayers

- Increased revenues for state government

- Increased local/parental control of schools

- Increased innovation in education. . . .

Lack of Funding Not the Problem

If funding was the problem for Illinois school children, where did all the money spent over the last 16–18 years go?

When confronted with this question at a 2005 debate on HB 750 [which would change tax and school funding laws, so

---

1. Charter schools receive public money but have different programs and accountability than most public schools. Students generally apply to or choose to attend charter schools.

schools would be funded by income taxes rather than by property taxes], the Honorable John Fritchey replied, "*Yeah, but that all went to pensions.*"

Where do you think the new spending is going? Does an early retirement benefit with a fat pension connect any neurons in a child's brain? If spending is the answer, how does it explain some results that we see right here in Illinois?

Study after study finds that there is little or no correlation between spending and educational outcomes.

Rich districts succeed because the parents are rich. The reforms we propose offer Illinois poor and disadvantaged access to the same outcomes. More money for the existing system does not.

There certainly are problems with Illinois schools, but lack of financial resources is not one of them. While there clearly is a "fairness issue," the source of that problem is Illinois' tax structure.

The so-called "Local Property Tax" for education is, in fact, a "*State Authorized*" tax. This means that though monies are taxed at the local level, the state can repeal all, or any portion, of the tax. This simple fact calls into question all the hand wringing over "funding disparities" in education. Illinois ranks 11th in school spending . . . , not 48th, as promoters of tax increases cynically argue. While there is a good argument to be made to fix Illinois structural problems, all recent proposals have been cynical ploys to raise taxes without any real reform.

HB 750 (and its various offspring SB 1484 and HB 755) is a *fictitious* tax swap that is promoted heavily by the Education Industry and many legislators. It calls for;

- A 67% increase in the Illinois income tax (from 3% to 5%)

- A 67% increase in the corporate income tax (from 4.8 to 8%)

- Expanding the sales-tax base to include all consumer services (e.g. Professional Fees, Home Cleaning and Maintenance)

Rather than promote a "swap" that leaves Illinois high property taxes in place to be raised again, the Fundamental Reform Plan recommends a *real tax swap* that zeros out the property tax for schools and replaces that money with state-based taxes.

A real "swap" will dramatically reduce the tax burden on millions of Illinois citizens while providing most of them with a substantial tax cut. With taxation and revenues for schools centralized in the entity with the Constitutional authority to provide "schooling," ([which is] the state), the overly complex barriers to reforming education are removed. . . .

Scholarships, Not Districts

Education in Illinois cannot be reformed at the margins. Where our schools "succeed," they do so at an unsustainable cost. Where they do not succeed, they are wasting not only vast sums of money, but vast quantities of human potential as well. The tax reform portion of our plan has empowered the state to assume its responsibility of funding education. It now requires the proper structure to meet that goal.

With new revenues going to the state ($8.5–9 billion in tax increases) added to existing state and federal funds used for education (about $9 billion), there will be enough money for the state *to fund every child in Illinois equally.* This offers Illinois an opportunity to end the egregious "education apartheid" fostered by the current tax structure.

Of course, the only way to guarantee that every child is funded equally, is to fund the child, and not systems, districts, and other bureaucratic structures. We propose that each child in Illinois receive a scholarship (around $7,000) that they can use at any Illinois school. To make such a proposal succeed, we need to:

- Phase out the "school district" as a governmental entity

- Convert every public school in Illinois into an independent "Charter School"

- Replace State Education Mandates with a system of annual, uniform, content-specific tests that show progress. . . .

Our reforms enhance "local control" by increasing school independence and parental choice. Conversely, state mandates prove that the current system provides the appearance, or the "myth of local control" without any of the decentralization that might actually serve Illinois citizens and children. The details of our plan separate the rhetoric of "local control" from the reality of allowing individual schools, and the parents that choose them, to decide what best serves their children.

It sounds like an outlandish question, but ask yourself, "Just what does a district do?" "What purpose does it serve?" Are Illinois schools paragons of local control? The answer is "no."

The idea that a school district is an independent entity is pretty much a myth. Our proposal calls for phasing out the school district as a governmental entity, and converting every Illinois public school to an independent Charter [School]. In the Fundamental Reform Plan we show that the district model provides next to zero "local control." We also show that funding children directly, (keep in mind that each child will receive a $7,000 scholarship) combined with the deregulation of individual schools, provides a level of local control and parental control that cannot exist in today's *bureaucracy-based* educa-

School Funding vs. Student Outcomes		
District in Illinois	Per Pupil Operating Expense	Percent of Students Who Meet or Exceed State Goals
Maine Township High School District	$13,617	67.2%
Washington Central District	$4,177	79.5%

TAKEN FROM: Bruno Behrend, "Executive Summary of a Plan For a Fundamental Reform of Illinois' Tax and Education Systems," n.d. [2006]. www.extremewisdom.com.

tion. That is why the "district" needs to be phased out, and every Illinois school converted to an independent Charter School. . . .

Charters Are More Effective

In a series of recent studies, Charter Schools have proven that they exceed or equal the results of the current unsustainable system at a lower cost. Caroline M. Hoxby and Jonah E. Rockoff, in a recently completed study of Chicago Charters found that:

> Our results demonstrate that, among students who enter in a typical grade, attending a charter school improves reading and math scores by an amount that is both statistically and substantively significant. We believe that these results can safely be extrapolated to similar schools that serve similar students. In particular, the results are most useful for understanding the effects of charter schools run by education-management organizations on student populations that comprise largely low-income and racial/ethnic minorities. We cannot confidently extrapolate the results to very different charter schools, students from very different backgrounds, or students who enter in atypical grades. Our re-

sults should be helpful for many policymakers who are concerned about urban students like those we study. However, we do not claim that the results are helpful for all policymakers.

Furthermore, there is a wide body of information available to parents on the best practices of Charter Schools, and how to find those that succeed. With such information in the hands of parents, their ability to choose schools will be far better than that of a faceless bureaucracy imposing its "one size fits all" model on them.

If every child is to receive a $7,000 scholarship, and every school is to become an independent Charter School, then how is the state going to manage the process of testing students and overseeing the schools?

Replace Standards for Testing

The Fundamental Reform Plan recommends *repealing all mandates and replacing them with a system of annual, uniform, content-specific tests covering a broad range of knowledge.*

Any school wishing to redeem scholarships must agree to meet these standards, while being allowed the *maximum amount of freedom of choice in the methods and curricula they use to attain them.* This structure will be a more effective measurement of student progress than the current ISAT [Illinois State Achievement Test] testing regime.

We further recommend that the process by which the tests are administered should be completely independent of the schools. This will remove most of the problems associated with "teaching to the test." Separating testing from the institutions providing the content will allow for more accurate measurement not only of teachers and schools, but of the testing institutions as well. . . .

Helping Children and Reducing Taxes

We recognize that the reforms discussed in this plan are aggressive. However, the time has come for such reforms. Illinois taxpayers deserve relief from the upward spiral of taxes and spending. Illinois school children deserve a better education than the one they are getting. . . .

In closing, we must stop worrying about teachers, their unions, the administrators, or their salaries and benefits. None of these things benefit Illinois children or taxpayers. "Funding Students and not Districts or Bureaucracies" must become the rallying cry (and the bedrock principle) underlying any and all aspects of education reform. . . . *This exercise is intended to change the focus of the debate [from] empowering parties, interests, and bureaucracies to empowering citizens and children.*

Hold in one hand a piece of paper representing your vote for an essentially powerless school board member in your district. Remember that their role is dictated by a state school code and enforced by a Superintendent that rose through the ranks of the education bureaucracy.

Hold in your other hand a $7,000 scholarship that allows you to choose the school that best suits your child's needs. Which provides you with the *illusion* of control and which better defines true control of your child's education?

As you ponder this question, think about a 50–65% reduction in your property tax.

| *"The tactics and rhetoric that teachers unions employ to block any meaningful reform is remarkable."*

Teachers' Unions Block School Reform

Center for Union Facts

The Center for Union Facts (CUF) is a nonprofit organization that gathers information about, and opposes the policies of, teachers' unions. In the following viewpoint, CUF argues that teachers' unions oppose school reform out of a financial interest in maintaining the status quo. CUF argues that teachers' unions are a major obstacle to initiating needed reforms such as merit pay, charter schools, and greater school choice. CUF concludes that unions put their own interest above the interest of students.

As you read, consider the following questions:

1. According to the author, how did a teachers' union prevent Detroit from receiving $200 million for charter schools?

2. What tactics did the California Teachers Association use to prevent a school-choice measure from reaching the ballot, according to *Forbes* magazine, as cited by the author?

3. As described by the author, what is "work to rule"?

Regardless of one's view of any particular method of improving America's struggling public schools (whether it's school choice, charter schools, or rewarding better teachers with better pay), the tactics and rhetoric that teachers unions employ to block any meaningful reform is remarkable. Their motivation is simple: maintain the status quo—and the flow of hundreds of millions of dollars in dues. Meanwhile, union leaders' suggestions for reform are best summarized as "more money to hire more teachers," who are then likely to become dues-paying union members.

Former top officers at the National Education Association's Kansas and Nebraska state chapters summarized their union's stance on reform in a 1994 issue of *Educational Freedom:* "The NEA has been the single biggest obstacle to education reform in this country. We know because we worked for the NEA."

Merit Pay and School Choice

Paying teachers according to how well they perform, a universal rule in the private sector, is consistently condemned by teachers unions. For example: When two-thirds of Los Angeles public schools received failing grades from the state of California in 2000, the superintendent announced his support for paying teachers according to merit. The United Teachers of Los Angeles (UTLA) fought this proposal tooth and nail and eventually killed it. Then-UTLA President Day Higuchi announced that the union would accept the reform only on "a cold day in hell."

Even when unions appear to be working to promote performance-based pay, their leaders may try to scuttle actual reform. When the *St. Petersburg Times* asked Pinellas Classroom Teachers Association executive director Jade Moore why few teachers were signing up for the merit pay program the union helped design for the school district, Moore replied, "Our goal was to make it nearly impossible."

Opposition to reform has even driven union bosses to reject hundreds of millions of dollars for public education—when those dollars pay for kids in non-unionized charter schools. In 2002 philanthropist Robert Thompson offered the city of Detroit $200 million to establish 15 charter schools. Until the fall of 2002, according to the *Detroit Free Press*, Michigan Governor Jennifer Granholm and Detroit Mayor Kwame Kilpatrick supported Thompson's offer. But on September 25 of that year, the Detroit Federation of Teachers led a one-day walkout that shut down the city's schools in protest of Thompson's offer. The deal collapsed immediately thereafter. . . .

Stronger medicine for public education brings even stronger anger from entrenched unions. The then-president of the California Teachers Association (CTA), the most powerful state teachers union in the country, gave an incredible rationalization for the extreme measures the union used in 1992 to prevent a school-choice measure from ever reaching Californians for a vote. "There are some proposals that are so evil that they should never even be presented to the voters," he said. He likened the proposed reform to legalizing the Ku Klux Klan and child prostitution.

Forbes magazine reported that the CTA took such a hardline stance against the ballot initiative in question that it used a variety of unheard-of tactics to keep the proposal off the ballot, including "blocking would-be signators' access to the petition in shopping malls, allegedly sabotaging the petition with fake names and offering a signature-collecting firm $400,000 to decline the account." . . .

Strangled by Union Contracts

In a windowless room in a shabby office building at Seventh Avenue and Twenty-eighth Street in Manhattan, a poster is taped to a wall, whose message could easily be the mission statement for a day-care center: "Children are fragile. Handle with care." It's a June morning, and there are fifteen people in the room. . . . But there are no children here. The inhabitants are all New York City schoolteachers who have been sent to what is officially called a Temporary Reassignment Center but which everyone calls the Rubber Room.

These fifteen teachers, along with about six hundred others, in six larger Rubber Rooms in the city's five boroughs, have been accused of misconduct, such as hitting or molesting a student, or, in some cases, of incompetence. . . .

The teachers have been in the Rubber Room for an average of about three years, doing the same thing every day—which is pretty much nothing at all. . . . They punch a time clock for the same hours that they would have kept at school—typically, eight-fifteen to three-fifteen. Like all teachers, they have the summer off. The city's contract with their union, the United Federation of Teachers, requires that charges against them be heard by an arbitrator, and until the charges are resolved—the process is often endless—they will continue to draw their salaries and accrue pensions and other benefits.

Steven Brill,
New Yorker, *August 31, 2009.*

Hurting Children

The New Jersey Education Association [NJEA], the most powerful teachers union in the state, vigorously opposed in 2008 a bill to provide tax credits for scholarships to allow low-income students to escape failing public classrooms. According to a Monmouth University poll, an overwhelming 74% majority of New Jersey residents supported the measure. Union officials declared the bill too costly to implement, but an independent taxpayers group found that the project would actually save the state more than $700 million while extending a lifeline to students trapped in underperforming and dangerous schools. Nor was this the first time that the NJEA opposed private-school scholarships for kids in need, as Andrew Coulson wrote in *Market Education*:

> In late October of 1995, officials of the Pepsi company announced at Jersey City Hall that their corporation would donate thousands of dollars in scholarships to help low-income children attend the private school of their choice. The immediate response of the local public school teachers' union was to threaten that a statewide boycott of all Pepsi products could not be ruled out. Pepsi vending machines around the city were vandalized and jammed. Three weeks later, company officials regretfully withdrew their offer. . . .

Upset with a policy change in 1992 that converted a half-hour of preparation time to instruction time in the seven-hour workday of D.C. public school teachers, the Washington Teachers Union called on teachers to ignore the new rule. When the district didn't budge, the *Washington Post* reported, teachers distributed letters to parents explaining that they would not write college recommendations for their children unless the parents and students took the union's side in its dispute with the reform proposal.

Known as "work to rule," this union slow-down tactic had D.C. teachers do only the work strictly required by their contracts and nothing else (such as writing recommendations, for example). With each recommendation request, parents were instructed to include union-supporting letters to three different office-holders, along with three addressed, stamped envelopes.

Influencing Policy

The control that teachers union officials can maintain over local school boards can verge on the ridiculous. Veteran education reporter Joe Williams wrote: "The United Teachers Los Angeles had such a tight grip on its school board in 2004 that union leaders actually instructed them on important policies and made no attempt to hide their hand signals to school board members during meetings."

With its corps of UniServ directors [who provide services to local unions], furthermore, the National Education Association (NEA) employs a larger number of political organizers than the Republican and Democratic National Committees combined—as Frederick Hess and Andrew Kelly point out, UniServ "has consistently been the NEA's most expensive budget item." UniServ directors assist local teachers unions with collective bargaining (supplying negotiation experience that often vastly outstrips the resources of a local school district), but they also serve as conduits for the union's political messages. Thanks to its UniServ network and its "member-to-member" communications, the NEA commands a get-out-the-vote network that's a powerful complement to its considerable political donations (and one that's nearly invisible to government oversight, too).

> *"I have always been puzzled by people who insist that the unions are the cause of everything that is wrong with education."*

Teachers' Unions Do Not Block School Reform

Diane Ravitch

Diane Ravitch is a research professor of education at New York University and a senior fellow at the Brookings Institution. In the following viewpoint, she argues that there is no evidence that schools without unions perform better than those with unions. She notes that it is possible to fire poorly performing teachers, even those with tenure. Unions, she concludes, simply guarantee teachers basic rights, such as the right not to be fired without due process and the right to have a voice in workplace conditions.

As you read, consider the following questions:

1. According to Ravitch, which high-performing school systems do not seem to be hampered by unions?

Diane Ravitch, "Unions Are Not the Problem," Blogs.edweek.org/EDweek/ Bridging-Differences, February 3, 2009. © 2009 Editorial Projects in Education. As first appeared on Edweek.org, February 3, 2009. Reprinted with permission from the author.

2. How many years must a teacher work in a school system before he or she obtains due process rights, according to Ravitch?

3. What percentage of the private sector workplace does Ravitch say is unionized?

On the subject of the teachers' unions, I must confess that I have always been puzzled by people who insist that the unions are the cause of everything that is wrong with education. If we only could get rid of the union, they say, then we could raise performance.

Blaming Unions Denies Facts

Recently, an old friend who is a businessman and philanthropist sent me a copy of a speech that he gave at [New York's TV] Channel 13's Celebration of Teaching and Learning. For many years, he and his family have very generously supported a school for gifted children in one of New York City's poorest neighborhoods. The main conclusion of his speech was that the obstacle to educating all children well is the union because the principal cannot hire and fire and assign teachers as he or she wants. He asked me what I thought of his ideas.

I responded that I was puzzled. The unions don't seem to cause low performance in the wealthy suburban districts that surround our city. They don't seem to be a problem for the nations that regularly register high scores on international tests. If getting rid of the unions was the solution to the problem of low performance, then why, I asked him, do the southern states—where unions are weak or non-existent—continue to perform worse than states with strong unions? And how can we explain the strong union presence in Massachusetts, which is the nation's highest performing state on NAEP [National Assessment of Educational Progress tests]? I suggested that low performance must be caused by something else other than teachers' unions. I have not yet received a reply, so I suppose he is thinking about it.

It actually doesn't seem to be all that hard to get rid of incompetent teachers. It appears that 40 percent of all those who enter teaching are gone within five years, according to research that I have seen. In every district, to my knowledge, teachers do not gain due process rights for three years (in some places, it takes five). During those three to five years, their supervisors have plenty of time and opportunity to evaluate them and tell them to leave teaching.

Then, when they have passed the three- or five-year mark, they have due process rights. They cannot be terminated without cause and due process. Although that is usually referred to as tenure, it really is not tenure. In higher education, tenure is an iron-clad guarantee of lifetime employment except for very egregious causes. Teachers do not have that. They have the right to due process. Many administrators would like to fire teachers without due process. I can't blame teachers for wanting protection from arbitrary administrators, especially now, when there are quite a few high-profile superintendents who like to grab headlines by threatening to fire teachers.

Teachers Need Union Protection

The right to form and join a union is one of the rights enumerated in the [United Nations'] Universal Declaration of Human Rights (Article 23). I made several trips to Eastern Europe and the Soviet Union before the end of the Cold War and met many teachers who were eager to belong to a union that would protect their interests. The state did not want unions or tolerated only faux unions.

I read recently that membership in unions is now under 10 percent of the private-sector workforce. Former Secretary of Labor Robert Reich wrote in the *Los Angeles Times* that the unions helped our nation build a solid middle class. Now, in

"Yes, I received the review copy of *Running a School Is a Snap* that you sent. I found it to be a very useful book." Cartoon by Aaron Bacall. www.cartoonstock.com.

these difficult times, we may again see a turn to unionism, and for all the predictable reasons, having to do with protection from arbitrary and capricious management to economic security to the demand to have a voice in decisions about the workplace.

By the way, I can't end without a suggestion: See *Slumdog Millionaire* [a 2008 film set in India]. It's the best movie I have seen in a long time, and it is successful without all that computer-generated fakery that we have grown accustomed to. I hope it wins the Oscar [*Slumdog Millionaire* won eight Academy Awards in 2009, including the award for Best Picture]. It is beautifully written, directed, and acted. And it shows us a world of grinding poverty, of life on the edge, of a struggle for survival. It also is a world without unions!

Periodical Bibliography

The following articles have been selected to supplement the diverse views presented in this chapter.

Mariah Blake	"Revisionaries: How a Group of Texas Conservatives Is Rewriting Your Kids' Textbooks," *Washington Monthly*, January–February 2010.
Thomas W. Carroll	"Teachers Unions Frequently Flunk School Reform Test," *New York Daily News*, August 5, 2009.
Kim Clark	"Will Obama's School Reform Plan Work?" *U.S. News & World Report*, December 9, 2009.
Chester E. Finn Jr.	"5 Myths About No Child Left Behind," *Washington Post*, March 30, 2008.
Nia-Malika Henderson	"New Course for No Child Left Behind," *Politico*, February 5, 2010. www.politico.com.
Joe Klein	"Why We're Failing Our Schools," *Time*, January 28, 2010.
Tom Loveless and Michael J. Petrilli	"Smart Child Left Behind," *New York Times*, August 27, 2009.
Terry M. Moe	"Change Our Public Schools Need," *Wall Street Journal*, November 24, 2008.
Andrew J. Rotherham	"In Politics of School Reform, Transparency Doesn't Equal Accountability," *U.S. News & World Report*, May 14, 2009.
Richard Stengal	"Arne Duncan: The Apostle of Reform," *Time*, April 15, 2009.
Greg Toppo	"Teachers Union Initiates School Reform Plan," *USA Today*, September 10, 2008.

CHAPTER 2

What Role Should Standardized Tests Play in Evaluating Students?

Chapter Preface

Since the early 2000s the federal government has mandated that states institute the testing of elementary and high school students. Each state, however, has significant latitude in what kinds of tests it wants to use and how the scores will be used.

California is the most populous state, and one with an extensive testing regime. California's testing system is known as the Standardized Testing and Reporting (STAR) program. The main tests used in STAR are the California Standards Tests (CSTs). According to the STAR Web site, these tests are administered from second to eleventh grade. The tests are mostly multiple choice, though in grade seven, students must also take a writing assessment. A September 2009 article on the Ed-Date Web site notes that CST exams are given in English, math, history/social studies, and science. Tests vary for each grade level, and they also vary in some cases based on what courses students are taking. The purpose of all of these tests is to assess student progress in relation to state standards.

In addition to the CSTs, California provides alternative tests for those with special circumstances. For instance, the Standards-based Tests in Spanish (STS) are used to measure the achievement of Spanish-speaking English learners. The California Alternate Performance Assessment (CAPA) is used to assess those students with learning disabilities that prevent them from taking the CSTs.

Besides those tests conducted through the STAR program, California also requires the California High School Exit Exam (CAHSEE). According to an article at GreatSchool.org, CAHSEE was instituted in 2006 and must be completed by all students in California. The test is multiple choice with an essay on a given topic. It covers math subjects, including Algebra I and statistics, and English subjects, including vocabulary and reading comprehension. CAHSEE is pass/fail, untimed and is first taken in tenth grade. Students who fail the exam are supposed to receive tutoring and additional classes to help them retake and pass the test. If students cannot pass the exam, they will not receive a high school diploma.

As noted previously, California's testing system is not the same as any other state's—for example, only about half the states require students to pass an exam in order to receive their high school diploma. However, looking at California does provide a sense of one way in which states conduct and use testing. The following viewpoints will look at the pros and cons of testing in California and throughout the country.

> *"Standardized multiple choice tests ...*
> *are and should be the primary instru-*
> *ment we use to measure student*
> *progress."*

Standardized Tests Are Needed to Measure Student Achievement

Patrick Mattimore

Patrick Mattimore is a journalist and a fellow at the Institute for Analytic Journalism. In the following viewpoint, he argues that standardized multiple choice tests are easy to administer and can provide quick, accurate, fair information about a student's ability to solve high-level problems. Mattimore concludes that the outcry against standardized testing is misguided, and that multiple choice tests should remain a primary means of assessing student achievement.

As you read, consider the following questions:

1. What Democratic presidential candidates does Mattimore say attacked testing in 2007?

2. According to the author, what are some of the things for which we use multiple choice tests?

3. What are the advantages of standardizing tests, according to Mattimore?

A t the National Education Association Representative Assembly in 2007, Democratic presidential contenders routinely lambasted the No Child Left Behind law [a 2002 school reform law], focusing largely on the testing requirements of the law.

Testing Does Not Prevent Teaching

Then [presidential] candidates President [Barack] Obama, Vice-President [Joseph] Biden, and Secretary of State [Hillary] Clinton all referred disparagingly to children filling in bubbles on standardized tests. Both Secretary Clinton and Vice-President Biden suggested that children were being forced to memorize things which, according to Secretary Clinton, got in the way of learning and, to Vice-President Biden's way of thinking, subverted critical thought. Secretary Clinton further opined that we were allowing our testing to drive our curriculum, rather than the other way around.

President Obama said that teachers had devoted themselves to teaching, not testing. Former Senator John Edwards pointed to the tee shirts that were being distributed at the Convention and repeated the shirt's message that a child was more than a test.

These sentiments all make sense but they are fundamentally flawed. The politicians' ideas imply an either/or situation when, in fact, standardized tests should go hand in hand with teaching. Testing and teaching are and must be conjoined. Each informs the other. Memorization is not inimical to either learning or critical thinking but is often the touchstone for those higher-order skills.

To many educators, standardized multiple choice tests are the wrong way to assess what our kids are learning. But those tests are and should be the primary instrument we use to measure student progress.

Multiple Choice Tests Work

Multiple choice tests are everywhere in America. They are the primary yardsticks in our K–12 assessments. Among other things, we use multiple choice tests for: college admissions; graduate school admissions; teacher licensing programs; licensing drivers, and; admission to professional practices, such as state bars [associations for practicing lawyers].

Multiple choice tests provide fast results, allowing teachers to provide immediate feedback and corrections. They are accurate, easy to administer and understand, objective, can be norm or criterion referenced, and most importantly, can test a variety of complexities of student knowledge.

To suggest that filling in bubbles is an endpoint of instruction misses the obvious point that the bubbling activity is a means for checking how well students are learning. Critics claim that the tests stifle creativity by forcing students to think in terms of right answers instead of possibilities, unfairly brand students, and measure only narrow ranges of ability.

But a well constructed multiple choice test will not only measure a student's retention of facts, but test that student's ability to apply what she has learned to novel problems and to make connections and inferences. A multiple choice test that incorporates a taxonomy of higher levels of thinking will force students to analyze, evaluate, and synthesize information.

Standardizing the tests insures that our students are being challenged on like measures and enables us to see across the board what is working and what is not. As an assessment measure, standardized multiple choice tests may not paint a student's complete academic portrait but they certainly provide us with a reasonable snapshot.

Secretary of Education Arne Duncan should insist upon standardized national assessment measures for all our students in every grade and those assessments should be primarily multiple choice.

Our elected representatives should disregard the educational reform chant that suggests that our current classroom deficiencies spring from the primary measures that help us diagnose our students' shortcomings. This is a classic case of shooting the messenger when what we should be doing is looking to that messenger to assist us in solving our educational problems.

> *"The assessments states have chosen to implement . . . are either nationally standardized achievement tests or state-developed standards-based tests—both of which are flawed."*

Standardized Tests Must Be Redesigned

W. James Popham

W. James Popham is professor emeritus at the University of California–Los Angeles School of Education and Information Studies. In the following viewpoint, he argues that the standardized tests used to evaluate students are deliberately designed to emphasize socioeconomic factors, and that they focus on an unmanageable number of goals and standards. As a result, raising scores on the exams is essentially impossible and forces teachers to adopt poor classroom practices. Popham concludes that policy makers must develop new tests that focus on fewer, more clearly defined tasks.

As you read, consider the following questions:

1. What did the Elementary and Secondary Education Act provide for and require, according to the author?

2. According to Popham, why do achievement test designers often link questions to socioeconomic status?

3. What three negative classroom consequences does the author claim result from using instructionally insensitive tests?

For the last four decades, students' scores on standardized tests have increasingly been regarded as the most meaningful evidence for evaluating U.S. schools. Most Americans, indeed, believe that students' standardized test performances are the only legitimate indicator of a school's instructional effectiveness.

The Tests Are Wrong

Yet, although test-based evaluations of schools seem to occur almost as often as fire drills, in most instances these evaluations are inaccurate. That's because the standardized tests employed are flat-out wrong.

Standardized tests have been used to evaluate America's schools since 1965, when the U.S. Elementary and Secondary Education Act [ESEA] became law. That statute provided for the first major infusion of federal funds into local schools and required educators to produce test-based evidence that ESEA dollars were well spent.

But how, you might ask, could a practice that's been so prevalent for so long be mistaken? Just think back to the many years we forced airline attendants and nonsmoking passengers to suck in secondhand toxins because smoking on airliners was prohibited only during takeoff and landing.

Some screw-ups can linger for a long time. But mistakes, even ones we've lived with for decades, can often be corrected once they've been identified, and that's what we must do to halt today's wrongheaded school evaluations. If enough educators—and noneducators—realize that there are serious flaws in the way we evaluate our schools, and that those flaws erode educational quality, there's a chance we can stop this absurdity.

First, some definitions:

A standardized test is any test that's administered, scored, and interpreted in a standard, predetermined manner. Standardized aptitude tests are designed to make predictions about how a test taker will perform in a subsequent setting. For example, the SAT [Scholastic Aptitude Test] and the ACT [American College Testing] are used to predict the grades that high school students will earn when they get to college. By contrast, standardized achievement tests indicate how well a test taker has acquired knowledge and mastered certain skills.

Although students' scores on standardized aptitude tests are sometimes unwisely stirred into the school-evaluation stew, scores on standardized achievement tests are typically the ones used to judge a school's success. Two kinds of standardized achievement tests commonly used for school evaluations are ill suited for that measurement.

The first of these categories are nationally standardized achievement tests like the Iowa Tests of Basic Skills, which employ a comparative measurement strategy. The fundamental purpose of all such tests is to compare a student's score with the scores earned by a previous group of test takers (known as the norm group). It can then be determined if Johnny scored at the 95th percentile on a given test (attaboy!) or at the tenth percentile (son, we have a problem).

Because of the need for nationally standardized achievement tests to provide fine-grained, percentile-by-percentile comparisons, it is imperative that these tests produce a considerable degree of score spread—in other words, plenty of differences among test takers' scores. So, producing score spread often preoccupies those who construct standardized achievement tests.

Statistically, a question that creates the most score spread on standardized tests is one that only about half the students answer correctly. Over the years, developers of standardized achievement tests have learned that if they can link students' success on a question to students' socioeconomic status (SES), then about half of the test takers usually answer that item correctly. If an item is answered correctly more often by students at the upper end of the socioeconomic scale than by lower-SES kids, that question will provide plenty of score spread.

After all, SES is a delightfully spread-out variable and one that isn't quickly altered. As a result, in today's nationally standardized achievement tests, there are many SES-linked items.

Unfortunately, this kind of test tends to measure not what students have been taught in school but what they bring to school. That's the reason there's such a strong relationship between a school's standardized-test scores and the economic and social makeup of that school's student body.

As a consequence, most nationally standardized achievement tests end up being instructionally insensitive. That is, they're unable to detect improved instruction in a school even when it has definitely taken place. Because of this insensitivity, when students' scores on such tests are used to evaluate a school's instructional performance, that evaluation usually misses the mark.

Standards-Based Tests

A second kind of instructionally insensitive test is the sort of standardized achievement test that many states have developed for accountability during the past two decades. Such tests have typically been created to better assess students' mastery of the officially approved skills and knowledge. Those skills and knowledge, sometimes referred to as goals or curricular aims, are usually known these days as content standards. Thus, such state-developed standardized assessments—like the Florida Comprehensive Assessment Test (FCAT)—are frequently described as standards-based tests.

Because these customized standards-based tests were designed (almost always with the assistance of an external test-development contractor) to be aligned with a state's curricular aspirations, it would seem that they would be ideal for appraising a school's quality. Unfortunately, that's not the way it works out.

When a state's education officials decide to identify the skills and knowledge students should master, the typical procedure for doing so hinges on the recommendations of subject-matter specialists from that state. For example, if authorities in Ohio or New Mexico want to identify their state's official content standards for mathematics, then a group of, say, 30 math teachers, math-curriculum consultants, and university math professors are invited to form a statewide content-standards committee.

Typically, when these committees attempt to identify the skills and knowledge students should master, their recommendation—not surprisingly—is that they should master everything. These committees seem bent on identifying skills they fervently wish students would possess. Regrettably, the resultant litanies of committee-chosen content standards tend to resemble curricular wish lists rather than realistic targets.

Whether or not the targets make sense, there tend to be a lot of them, and the effect is counterproductive. A state's standards-based tests are intended to evaluate schools based on students' test performances, but teachers soon become overwhelmed by too many targets. Educators must guess about which of this multitude of content standards will actually be assessed on a given year's test. Moreover, because there are so many content standards to be assessed and only limited testing time, it is impossible to report any meaningful results about which content standards have and haven't been mastered.

After working with standards-based tests aimed at so many targets, teachers understandably may devote less and less attention to those tests. As a consequence, students' performances on this type of instructionally insensitive test often become dependent on the very same SES factors that compromise the utility of nationally standardized achievement tests when used for school evaluation.

The Negative Results of Poor Tests

Bad things happen when schools are evaluated using either of these two types of instructionally insensitive tests. This is particularly true when the importance of a school evaluation is substantial, as it is now. All of the nation's public schools are evaluated annually under the provisions of the federal No Child Left Behind Act [NCLB, a 2002 school reform law].

Not only are the results of the NCLB school-by-school evaluations widely disseminated, there are also penalties for schools that receive NCLB funds yet fail to make sufficient test-based progress. These schools are placed on an improvement track that can soon "improve" them into nonexistence. Educators in America's public schools obviously are under tremendous pressure to improve their students' scores on whatever NCLB tests their state has chosen.

With few exceptions, however, the assessments states have chosen to implement because of NCLB are either nationally standardized achievement tests or state-developed standards-based tests—both of which are flawed. Here, then, are three adverse classroom consequences seen in states where instructionally insensitive NCLB tests are used:

Curricular Reductionism

In an effort to boost their students' NCLB test scores, many teachers jettison curricular content that—albeit important—is not apt to be covered on an upcoming test. As a result, students end up educationally shortchanged.

Excessive Drilling

Because it is essentially impossible to raise students' scores on instructionally insensitive tests, many teachers—in desperation—require seemingly endless practice with items similar to those on an approaching accountability test. This dreary drilling often stamps out any genuine joy students might (and should) experience while they learn.

Modeled Dishonesty

Some teachers, frustrated by being asked to raise scores on tests deliberately designed to preclude such score raising, may be tempted to adopt unethical practices during the administration or scoring of accountability tests. Students learn that whenever the stakes are high enough, the teacher thinks it's OK to cheat. This is a lesson that should never be taught.

These three negative consequences of using instructionally insensitive standardized tests as measuring tools, taken together, make it clear that today's widespread method of judging schools does more than lead to invalid evaluations. Beyond that, such tests can dramatically lower the quality of education.

What Should Be Done

Is it possible to build accountability tests that both supply accurate evidence of school quality and promote instructional improvement? The answer is an emphatic yes. In 2001, prior to the enactment of NCLB, an independent national study group, the Commission on Instructionally Supportive Assessment, identified three attributes an "instructionally supportive" accountability test must possess:

A Modest Number of Supersignificant Curricular Aims

To avoid overwhelming teachers and students with daunting lists of curricular targets, an instructionally supportive accountability test should measure students' mastery of only an intellectually manageable number of curricular aims, more like a half-dozen than the 50 or so a teacher may encounter today. However, because fewer curricular benchmarks are to be measured, they must be truly significant.

Problems with Teaching to the Test

Many observers worry that drill-focused forms of teaching to the test can crowd out opportunities to teach students more advanced cognitive skills, such as how to solve problems and communicate effectively. They point to the work of economists, such as Frank Levy and Richard Murnane, who warn that all kinds of jobs, but particularly higher paying jobs, increasingly require fewer rote and routine skills and ever more complex skills. Analyzing tasks performed in jobs across the economy between 1969 and 1999, . . . Levy and Murnane found a big decline in rote tasks and routine work along with a skyrocketing demand for "expert thinking" skills (the ability to solve problems that require more than simply following rules or applying knowledge to new situations) and "complex communication" skills.

Craig D. Jerald,
Center for Comprehensive School Reform and Improvement,
July 2006.

Lucid Descriptions of Aims

An instructionally helpful test must be accompanied by clear, concise, and teacher-palatable descriptions of each curricular aim to be assessed. With clear descriptions, teachers can direct their instruction toward promoting students' mastery of skills and knowledge rather than toward getting students to come up with correct answers to particular test items.

Instructionally Useful Reports

Because an accountability test that supports teaching is focused on only a very limited number of challenging curricular aims, a student's mastery of each subject can be meaningfully measured, letting teachers determine how effective their instruction has been. Students and their parents can also benefit from such informative reports.

These three features can produce an instructionally supportive accountability test that will accurately evaluate schools and improve instruction. The challenge before us, clearly, is how to replace today's instructionally insensitive accountability tests with better ones. Fortunately, at least one state, Wyoming, is now creating its own instructionally supportive NCLB tests. More states should do so.

If you want to be part of the solution to this situation, it's imperative to learn all you can about educational testing. Then learn some more. For all its importance, educational testing really isn't particularly complicated, because its fundamentals consist of commonsense ideas, not numerical obscurities.

You'll not only understand better what's going on in the current mismeasurement of school quality, you'll also be able to explain it to others. And those others, ideally, will be school board members, legislators, and concerned citizens who might, in turn, make a difference. Simply hop on the Internet or head to your local library and hunt down an introductory book or two about educational assessment. (I've written several such books that, though not as engaging as a crackling good spy thriller, really aren't intimidating.)

With a better understanding of why it is so inane—and destructive—to evaluate schools using students' scores on the wrong species of standardized tests, you can persuade anyone who'll listen that policy makers need to make better choices. Our 40-year saga of unsound school evaluation needs to end. Now.

"Teacher observations and standardized tests should each play a role in a well-rounded system for assessing our students."

Standardized Tests Alone Should Not Be Used to Evaluate Students

Bill Ferriter

Bill Ferriter teaches sixth grade language arts in Wake County, North Carolina, where he was named Teacher of the Year for 2005–2006. In the following viewpoint, he discusses his visit to Denmark, where standardized testing is deemphasized in favor of an examination that focuses on discussion and qualitative assessment. Ferriter argues that the Danish example shows that the United States has come to overemphasize standardized tests. He concludes that the United States needs to move back to valuing teacher expertise in assessing student progress.

As you read, consider the following questions:

1. What do classroom teachers put together for the Danish exams that Ferriter observed?

Bill Ferriter, "Assessing Learning the Danish Way," *The Tempered Radical*, June 21, 24, 2009. Reproduced by permission of the author.

2. Why were Ferriter's Danish friends shocked that the United States begins giving exams in third grade?

3. In the parent-teacher conference Ferriter discusses, what evidence did he use to provide an assessment of the student?

As most [*Tempered*] *Radical* readers know, I've spent the past eight days [in June 2009] touring Denmark as a part of a program run by the Center for International Understanding—one of North Carolina's most important professional development organizations for teachers.

While I completely enjoyed the opportunities that I had to learn more about the European Union and Denmark's social welfare system—topics that are a part of the curriculum that I teach—my favorite experience of the entire week was observing two different students go through the only official examination that generations of Danish children have ever taken, which comes at the end of tenth grade.

Student Exams in Denmark

Kind of geeky, huh? I mean who spends the better part of 8 days in a 1,000-year old land full of history, cultural geography and really good beer observing tenth grade final exams?!

The thing that drew me to the testing room—besides the fact that exams are public events that can be observed by anyone (including parents and community leaders) who asks for permission ahead of time—was that Denmark's final exams are probably the most responsible system of student assessment that I've ever seen in action.

Here's how they go:

1. Classroom teachers put together a collection of readings and audio recordings related to content studied during the course of the school year. In the sessions that I ob-

served—both English exams—there were packets of materials on 20 different topics ranging from racism and role models to terrorism and global warming.

2. Also included was a list of related lessons that students had completed on the topic in their regular classes. These lists included things like articles read, videos watched, and seminars completed. While the supporting materials for each lesson were not included, these lists allowed students to dig into their background knowledge while attacking new texts.

3. Each student arrived at a pre-scheduled time, entered the examination room and randomly selected a number corresponding to one of the predetermined topics. Then, he/she spent twenty minutes studying the new materials: taking notes, filling out reading guides, listening to recordings, and planning a personal response to the topic that they'd selected.

4. After 20 minutes—a time period that was closely monitored—the student returned to the assessment room where his/her classroom teacher was waiting with a teacher of the same grade level from a school in a nearby town. The rest of the assessment consisted of an ongoing conversation between the student and the assessors about the topic selected.

5. The assessors carefully listened to each student, looking for evidence of reflective thinking and for the ability to connect new texts to previous materials or experiences. While students did the majority of the talking during the 20-minute assessment period, both assessors asked prodding questions to challenge students and to test the depth of their knowledge about the topic selected.

6. When the students finished working through their thoughts, they were asked to leave the examination

room. Then, the assessors—guided by a predetermined rubric—engaged in a 10-minute conversation with one another to determine the student's level of mastery.

7. To ensure that final scores weren't biased, the outside assessor—who had no relationship with the student being tested—took the lead in the conversation and in determining the score given, but both teachers interacted with each other and came to general consensus around each bullet point on the rubric. If there had been disagreement, the school principal would have been called in to determine a final score.

8. Finally, the student returned to the room to receive feedback from both teachers. Suggestions for future work were offered, compliments were given, and the final score was awarded.

Kind of amazing, huh? And remember that until recently— *Denmark has instituted a much smaller system of standardized testing within the last two years that is designed to give quick feedback to teachers, principals and parents*—this was the only "end of grade exam" that Danish kids had to suffer through!

Quite honestly, my Danish friends who teach are completely shocked that we begin giving exams to students in third grade here in the States. They can't understand what we think we can learn from tests that we can't already learn from a teacher's year-long observation of a student's performance in the classroom. . . .

Standardized Tests Are Overvalued

Teacher observations and standardized tests should each play a role in a well-rounded system for assessing our students. . . . Assessment should never be an either/or proposition. Instead, we should get our hands on as much information as possible when trying to diagnose a course of action for our kids.

The problem ... is that American schools *have* made student assessment an either/or proposition. Teacher observations have become increasingly irrelevant as districts and states try to meet the testing targets set by the No Child Left Behind legislation [a 2002 federal school reform law].

Let me give you an example of how this shift has played out in my classroom: Not long ago, I had a parent ask for a conference to learn more about her son's abilities in my language arts classroom. Having had a great relationship with her boy over the course of the year, I knew his strengths and weaknesses better than I knew the strengths and weaknesses of most of the kids who roll through my classroom, so I was looking forward to our meeting.

During our time together, I went into great detail with this mother, providing writing samples that highlighted strengths and weaknesses, reviewing classroom assessments that had caused struggle, and sharing observations about verbal ability and vocabulary based on countless interactions over the entire year. I actually felt pretty darn good about the "assessment" that I'd made of my student.

The first words [his] mother said when I was finished: "That's all great, but what does the test say?"

Teacher Expertise Is Important

With nine simple words, she'd completely dismissed my professional opinion, opting instead for the cold, hard, *seemingly more accurate* facts. And when you look at the kind of weight we place on standardized tests as a tool for measuring everything from student performance to school quality, it seems like pushing the professional opinions of classroom teachers to the sideline has become common practice.

So I guess that's why I'm drawn to a system of assessment that places teacher observations first, ... While I'm all for standardized tests that are used to diagnose student strengths and weaknesses, *I think we've moved beyond using standardized tests for diagnosis in our country.* Instead, standardized tests have become our primary tool for evaluation and accountability—of students, of teachers and of schools. . . .

Will we ever get back a comfortable—and professional—middle ground where teacher observations are paired with diagnostic tests to paint a clear picture of what our students know and can do?

> "Youth of color, those who speak English as a second language or who have a disability or are from low-income families are disproportionately denied a diploma because of a test score."

Standardized Tests Are Unfair and Harmful

Monty Neill

Monty Neill is director of the National Center for Fair and Open Testing (FairTest). In the following viewpoint he argues that high-stakes testing is a poor measure of student ability. He contends that testing hurts students by increasing drop-out rates, making students repeat grades, and forcing teachers to teach to the test. Since testing occurs disproportionately in African-American and Latino schools, he maintains, it unfairly undermines minority education.

As you read, consider the following questions:

1. According to Neill, which states do not have graduation tests, and what is the makeup of their student populations?

2. What does the term "education debt" mean, as used by the author?

3. In Neill's opinion, how have graduation rates and number of dropouts been affected by the institution of high-stakes testing in California and Texas?

On the campaign trail, President [Barack] Obama declared, "We should not be forced to spend the academic year preparing students to fill in bubbles on standardized tests," and he called for "a broader range of assessments that can evaluate higher-order skills." The nation and its students need assessments in all the important areas, both so the public knows what is happening in schools and to avoid narrowing curriculum and instruction to fit tests that cannot indicate real success and readiness for future learning.

Growth of Standardized Tests

If the nation's goal is a high-quality education for all, why not use assessments that can at least tell us if that goal is being met? Why not rely on multiple sources of evidence to inhibit narrowing curriculum and teaching to one test format? Why not make decisions about students and schools based on information gathered over time? Why not transform assessment and accountability to serve the educational needs of all students? A truly healthy educational system will prioritize high-quality classroom instruction and use school-based assessment information to monitor classroom, school and district progress. Sadly, the nation's public education system does not function that way.

Standardized tests have been prevalent for much of the latter half of the 20th century. The emphasis on standardized testing has intensified in recent decades as elected officials, business leaders and others have fostered the idea that the U.S. economy will decline unless student achievement and school progress is increasingly monitored through testing.

In 2002, former President George W. Bush won passage of the No Child Left Behind Act (NCLB), pushing the emphasis on multiple-choice, paper-and-pencil tests to new heights. Under NCLB, an ever-escalating percentage of students in every public school and district is expected to score at a proficient level on statewide standardized tests each year. Students as a whole and also specific ethnic and racial groups must meet this "Adequate Yearly Progress" (AYP) requirement.

The pressure to pass standardized tests intensified dramatically under NCLB. Schools that repeatedly fail to make AYP face escalating sanctions, culminating in "restructuring," which can include replacing a school's staff or turning it over to private management. Schools that have struggled the most to make AYP are those with the highest percentages of poor students, which typically have fewer resources. In these schools, teachers are frequently expected to rigidly "deliver" a pre-programmed, often tightly scripted curriculum, each day covering a set of skills to prepare students for the tests. Teachers often lack the authority to deviate from the mandated curriculum regardless of student needs, emerging issues or the teachers' recognition that these curricula fail to prepare students for future success. School staff fear that without narrowing the curriculum and tailoring the instruction to fit the tests, their students fare poorly, putting the students themselves and their schools at risk of severe sanctions.

Testing Minorities

One risk students face in a majority of states is the graduation test. These tests began in Florida in the late 1970s. A lawsuit delayed the use of the graduation test on the grounds that many Black students had not had a fair opportunity to learn the material on which they were tested because they had attended schools segregated by law. The courts ruled that once students that had begun school after the end of de jure [legal] segregation had graduated, the tests could be used. This ruling ignored the extensive de facto [actual] segregation and the vastly disparate resources available to Blacks and Whites.

Graduation tests quickly spread across the South and then to northern states with large populations of students of color in their cities, such as New York, Ohio and New Jersey. In 1995–96, 11 of 16 states in the Southern Regional Education Board had exit exams, compared with only six of the remaining 35 states (including DC). Those states also tested an average of 7.5 grades, substantially higher than the national average of 5.28 grades. In effect, the worst-performing systems and those with the highest proportions of African Americans, were most likely to implement high-stakes testing.

The next wave of states to enact graduation tests—after a mid-1990s halt in the growth of such tests—were disproportionately Latino. New Mexico and Texas, which imposed exit exams in the first wave, were joined by Arizona and California, for example. States with tests comprise about 70 percent of the nation's student population, but over 80 percent of its African-American and Latino students. The states without graduation tests form a belt from Illinois to Idaho, and north of Oklahoma—and in most cases have predominantly White student populations. Thus, there is clearly a racial dimension to the use of graduation exams, and youth of color, those who speak English as a second language or who have a disability or are from low-income families are disproportionately denied a diploma because of a test score.

The same is just as true for tests students must pass to move to the next grade, which are found in Florida, Louisiana, Texas and many large cities, such as Chicago and New York. As with diploma denial, the damage of grade retention falls disproportionately on youth of color. Extensive research has demonstrated that students who are held back progress more slowly than comparable students who are promoted, they suffer significant loss of self-esteem, and they are far more likely to not graduate. . . .

Education Debt

The interaction of under-resourced schools and testing most powerfully hits students of color. They are disproportionately denied diplomas or grade promotion, and the schools they attend are the ones most likely to fare poorly on the tests and face sanctions such as restructuring.

Professor Gloria Ladson-Billings uses the term "education debt" to explain the lack of adequate educational opportunity for African-American students accumulating since slavery and segregation. She thinks that focusing on this inequality is far more meaningful than the commonly used "achievement gap," which only refers to unequal test results. The debt includes the school-based debt in resources. It also includes the housing debt that forced people of color to suffer inferior living conditions, exemplified by the racial covenants that ensured African Americans could not move to many suburbs after World War II. Ladson-Billings speaks also of the medical care debt, the pervasive historical and current unequal access to medical care by race, and the employment debt—African-American families earn three-fifths of what White families earn while U.S. income inequality grows rapidly.

Test-based "school reform" such as NCLB, which passed with support from both Democrats and Republicans, is an effort to improve results while ignoring the existence of the education debt.

The tools used to improve results—tests and sanctions—actually make things worse. Low-income students, who are disproportionately children of color, go to under-resourced schools that serve up a thin gruel of test preparation. So long as such a system remains in place, the pipeline to college and good jobs for low-income and minority-group youths will remain narrow, but the pipe-lines to prison and unemployment will remain wide.

High-stakes testing undermines school quality. What is it about the use of standardized tests as the primary, even sole, arbiter of school quality that is problematic? Partly it is because, in the face of escalating sanctions, some schools and districts have taken harmful actions such as increasing suspensions and expulsions of low scorers—removing perceived problem kids from the classrooms instead of dealing with their problems. And partly it is the damage done to teaching.

Testing's control over teaching is unevenly applied. The drill-and-kill school practices that guarantee students will not be ready for college, skilled employment, lifelong learning or effective citizenship are most prevalent in schools serving low-income children of color. No one has documented this more powerfully than Jonathan Kozol in *Shame of the Nation*. Building on his earlier exposé, *Savage Inequalities*, of the vastly unequal opportunities provided in different communities across the nation, Kozol describes in painful detail the brain-deadening, emotionally stultifying consequences of scripted curricula and test preparation in what he terms "apartheid education."

Suburban middle- and upper-class schools succumb to a degree to teaching to state exams, but teaching to the test is nowhere near as prevalent or powerful in those communities. And the suburban schools certainly do not employ the tightly scripted curricula widely used in urban schools.

The learning gaps revealed by standardized tests mask worse gaps in more advanced learning skills. For example, students in well-to-do schools typically learn to write research papers, which colleges expect students to do. There are no research papers on standardized tests. If the primary goal is to boost test scores ..., teachers will not take time out to teach needed research and writing skills. As noted psychologist Robert Sternberg wrote, "The increasingly massive and far-reaching use of conventional standardized tests is one of the most effective, if unintentional, vehicles this country has created for suppressing creativity." That suppression, too, most powerfully affects students who are most subject to the tests.

Unsuccessful Testing Preparation

In a New York City middle school, the principal asked teachers to spend fifteen minutes a day with students practicing how to answer multiple-choice math questions in preparation for the state-mandated test. One teacher protested, explaining she taught Italian and English, not math. But the principal insisted, and she followed his directive. . . . In the end, fewer than one in four New York City middle schoolers passed the exam. . . . Students learned that test scores mattered more than English or Italian. . . . In fact once the test was over, one-third of the students in her class stopped attending school, skipping the last five weeks of the school year.

David Miller Sadker and Karen R. Zittleman,
Education, 2009. www.education.com.

Tests Lower Graduation Rates

With tests as one key factor, African-American and Latino graduation rates barely reach 60 percent. The consequences are severe. Non-graduates have significantly lower lifetime earnings and less stable families; they are more likely to be unemployed or imprisoned. Graduation rates for low-achieving minority students and girls have fallen nearly 20 percentage points since California implemented high school exit exams, according to "Effects of the California High School Exit Exam on Student Persistence, Achievement, and Graduation," a research paper published by Stanford University's Institute for Research on Education Policy and Practice. In 2007–08, 40,000 more students failed to graduate than did so in pre-test years.

Similarly, more than 40,000 Texas students were denied diplomas in 2007 because they did not pass all four parts of the state's graduation exam. These casualties are a direct result of high-stakes accountability systems designed to maximize test scores.

Current research by John Robert Warren and his colleagues clearly demonstrates that graduation tests increase the number of dropouts, do not lead to improved test scores, and do not produce better results in college or employment. They are, in effect, wholly negative.

The Standards for Educational and Psychological Testing, produced by the American Educational Research Association, American Psychological Association, and National Council on Measurement in Education, warn against these practices: "[A] decision . . . that will have major impact on a student should not be made on the basis of a single test score." Similarly, the American Evaluation Association concludes, "High stakes testing leads to under-serving or mis-serving all students, especially the most needy and vulnerable, thereby violating the principle of 'do no harm'." Policy makers have ignored the wisdom of the very people who make, use and research tests.

Civil rights organizations have long battled these make or break tests. They point out that systems that deny diplomas or promotions based on test scores typically fail to provide an adequate or equitable opportunity to all students to learn the material on which students are tested. This places the burden of accountability on the backs of children, hitting children with the worst education systems and the fewest resources hardest.

African-American and Latino children are more frequently retained in grades than are Whites. In Chicago in 2008, 98.6% of Whites passed the grade promotion test, compared with 85.5% of African Americans. These disparities have not changed much over the years. Since 2002, 12.9% of Chicago's

Black students have been held back while only 2.3% of Whites have faced the same fate. In 2008, 5.4% of Latinos were retained.

Chicago-based researchers evaluated the consequences and concluded that retention is harmful. Retained students did less well academically than comparable students who were promoted, and retention increased the likelihood of dropping out. . . .

The Chicago studies confirmed decades of previous research showing that flunking students diminishes their self-esteem, reduces their likelihood of graduation, and fails to increase achievement. Because grade retention is harmful and test-based policies lead to more retention overall with disproportionate increases for African Americans and Latinos, test-based retention intensifies race-based inequalities in school systems, such as Chicago's public schools.

There is a ready solution to the "social promotion" versus "retention" dispute: promote students, but provide intensive extra support to those who are not doing well, as soon as academic problems are identified. Providing such support would help schools avoid inflicting the damage of retention while being able to offer the help many students need. Helpful support would focus not on boosting test scores but on strengthening real academic knowledge and skills.

Good Assessment Is Essential

A good assessment—understanding what has been learned and student learning processes—is essential for teaching and learning. It is also a core component of holding students, teachers, schools and districts accountable for their work, class time and resources. While the processes of assessment and accountability often overlap, they do not go hand in hand. Many assessments used in education have nothing to do with accountability. And demonstrating a student's, teacher's or school's success, in short, accountability, should involve far more than academic assessments.

In *Grading Education: Getting Accountability Right,* authors Richard Rothstein, Rebecca Jacobsen, and Tamara Wilder wrote that their research showed that the general public, legislators and school board members view the purposes of education broadly and think it should serve many purposes, including the teaching of: academics, critical thinking, arts and literature, preparation for skilled work, social skills, work ethics, citizenship, physical health, and emotional health. Other researchers have come up with similar results.

In "Empowering Schools and Improving Learning," the Forum on Educational Accountability [FEA] proposes accountability structures that would look at inputs, what students are getting on the front end, including the quality of health care and housing in addition to teacher quality and school resources. FEA proposes that schools and districts collaborate with families and communities to meet the needs of the whole child—cognitive/intellectual, social, civic, emotional, psychological, ethical, and physical—while preparing them for successful citizenship in a multicultural world.

Assessments should include multiple kinds of evidence, from multiple-choice questions to essays and projects, teacher observations and student self-evaluations. Good teachers know how to use a broad range of assessments and that one can use many different tools to assess knowledge. Unfortunately, pressure to boost scores on standardized tests has reduced the range of assessments teachers use. For example, one teacher, in a FairTest report on NCLB, described how she had to reduce the number of book reports she assigned because of the time required for test prep. These kinds of stories have been told thousands of times across the nation.

Teachers use high quality assessment results to adjust their teaching ("formative" assessing) and to evaluate student success ("summative" assessing). This means that good teachers use a variety of measures to gather a great deal of evidence about student learning. Most of the time, this evidence stops with the teacher. It may show up as a grade, or in a discussion with parents or next year's teacher, but it rarely informs efforts to improve schools or shape policy or provide public accountability. In short, a much richer sampling of learning is ignored in favor of a narrow set of data called test scores.

"The majority of ELLs do not perform as well as native English speakers on the standardized tests."

Standardized Tests in English Are Unfair to ESL Students

Kate Menken

Kate Menken is an assistant professor of linguistics at Queens College of the City University of New York and a former teacher of English as a second language. In the following viewpoint, she argues that high-stakes testing hurts English Language Learners (ELLs) by forcing them to retake tests, extending their schooling, and increasing their drop-out rates. She notes that this is the case even for the best ELL students, who have completed coursework, and who may even have been accepted into college, but who cannot proceed because of the difficulty in passing the standardized tests.

As you read, consider the following questions:

1. As reported by Menken, what unexpected outcomes did Amrein and Berliner find high-stakes testing associated with?

2. In 2005, what percentage of ELLs passed the English Regents exam, and what percentage of all students did so, according to the author?

3. According to Menken, what are some reasons that ELLs systematically stay in school beyond the traditional four years?

Most states in the United States are now administering standardized tests, and using the results to make crucial decisions about individual students.... ELLs [English Language Learners, or students who do not speak English as their first language] are particularly vulnerable to high-stakes decisions based on test results. Tests are used to determine high school graduation, grade promotion and the placement of ELLs into tracked or remedial education programs. The supporters of high-stakes testing and the accountability mandates of No Child Left Behind [NCLB, a 2002 federal school reform law] argue that these policies will improve the education of poor and minority students and reduce the achievement gap, while opponents of these policies argue instead that their effects are punitive for these students and in fact reduce the quality of education they receive....

Negative Consequences of Testing

[Researchers Audrey] Amrein and [David] Berliner note a number of the unintended consequences of high-stakes testing for student academic performance, in their study of testing data from 28 states. They found high-stakes testing to be associated with:

- Increased dropout rates, decreased graduation rates, and higher rates of younger individuals taking the Graduate Equivalency Diploma (GED)[equivalent to a high school diploma] exams;

- Higher numbers of low performing students being retained in grade before pivotal testing years to ensure their preparedness; and,

- High numbers of suspensions and expulsions of low performing students before testing days. These findings support many of the concerns raised by educators and educational researchers with regard to negative outcomes of high-stakes testing for all students, and particularly ELLs.

A major critique of test-based accountability systems increasingly visible in the literature is that the tests fail language minority youth. [Researchers Angela] Valenzuela and [Linda] McNeil . . . find support for many of the findings above in their exploration of the impact of high-stakes testing in Texas. Praised by politicians and gaining national recognition for raising educational quality, these authors find instead that "Texas-style accountability," the model upon which No Child Left Behind is based, reduces the quality and quantity of education offered, and has the most damaging effects on poor and minority youth. While scores have increased on statewide tests overall, the vast majority of students failing these high-stakes exams are African Americans, Latinos, and English language learners (ELLs). . . .

Many states are now implementing high school exit exams that also serve to meet the accountability requirements of No Child Left Behind. . . . According to a study by the Center on Education Policy . . . , 20 states are using high school exit exams to also meet NCLB high school requirements and they predict that 87% of ELLs will have to pass high school exit exams in the near future. As they write:

Almost all states with exit requirements have an implicit requirement that students should know English in order to graduate from high school. Consistent with this, ELLs must generally pass state exit exams in reading/language arts in English. . . .

In this way, these authors draw a link between testing policy and language policy that promotes English; having English-only testing as a graduation requirement is tantamount to English-only policy.

On the other side of the testing debate, however, supporters of No Child Left Behind accountability mandates state that the law is critical for closing the achievement gap among students according to race, class and ethnicity.

> "There is a battle raging for the soul of American education," noted Kati Haycock, Director of The Education Trust. "In our work around the country, we often hear local educators talk about the progress they are seeing *as a result of* the new accountability. These education leaders are especially concerned with the messages communicated by those opposed to accountability. Too often, the critics imply that students from low-income families and students of color simply cannot be expected to be taught to high levels." . . .

Leaders of the Education Trust argue that the law has brought the needs of low-performing students into the public spotlight, causing greater attention to be paid to these students then before. The findings presented below indicate that while attention towards these students has indeed increased, much of that attention has been negative.

ELLs Retaking Tests

In New York City and elsewhere across the United States, the majority of ELLs do not perform as well as native English speakers on the standardized tests being used for accountability purposes under No Child Left Behind. . . . Because of the traditionally poorer performance by ELLs on Regents exams [New York statewide exams that students must pass to graduate] and because the tests are attached to the attainment of a high school diploma, these findings show that English lan-

Comparison of English Language Learners (ELLs) Pass Rates to Overall Pass Rates on English and Math A Regents Exams, By Year

Exam	Year	Overall pass rate	ELL pass rate	ELL differential
English Regents	2002	74.2%	17.4%	−56.8%
	2003	75.2%	32.5%	−42.7%
	2004	80.7%	36.2%	−44.5%
	2005	77.9%	33.2%	−44.7%
Math A Regents	2002	50.8%	28.4%	−22.4%
	2003	59.5%	36.3%	−23.2%
	2004	86.9%	58.1%	−28.8%
	2005	81.5%	55.5%	−26.0%

Department of Education, Division of Assessment and Accountability (2003b, 2004a, 2005). The Regents exams are required New York State exams.

TAKEN FROM: Kate Mencken, *English Learners Left Behind: Standardized Testing As Language Policy*, Bristol, UK: Multilingual Matters, 2008, p. 44.

guage learners are greatly impacted by the exams every day. For an English language learner in high school, high-stakes standardized exams are therefore a major part of their introduction and enculturation to the United States, given that they are such a defining force in students' daily educational experiences. . . .

ELLs often take Regents exams over and over again, in an effort to increase their scores and pass. . . . I spoke with students in many schools whose sole reason for returning to high school each day was to increase their test scores to the minimum required to pass. Below are two excerpts from interviews showing how prevalent it is for ELLs to retake exams, the first from a student focus group at one school and the second from an interview with an assistant principal at another school:

[Excerpt One:]

[*"S2" is from Bangladesh, "S3" is from Guinea and "S4" is from the Dominican Republic. They are 11th or 12th graders ... and recent arrivals to the United States*]

How do you feel about the Regents exams? Are they important? Why or why not?

... S3: Some of us started in 11th grade. They put the Regents for everybody, like everybody knows English. But I only been here two years, so I had to take each of the Regents twice before I passed it.

S4: I took biology twice and still haven't passed it. It's really hard.

S2: English Regents is hardest for all of us.

S4: Yeah, it's six hours!

S2: People born here and stuff it's easy for them, but for us it's really hard. The math and stuff isn't hard but the English is.

S3: English is the hardest because most of the kids take English Regents four or five times before they pass—not the regular English kids, but the ESL [English as a second language] kids. The first time I failed with a 36, and the second time I passed. It's not really that easy, man. . . . The Regents also slows us up. If we don't pass in June, I'm 18 and we have to stay here. . . .

[Excerpt Two:] (Ms. V., Assistant Principal of Instruction)

How are the standardized tests affecting your ELL students, and what are the greatest challenges of the tests for ELLs?

Ms. V: . . . Overall I have about 60% of ELLs meeting the benchmark of 55 and higher on the English Regents. I don't know, I think the schoolwide average is 73 or 78? I'm blank-

ing. But anyway, there are 60% meeting it at any given time.
But to graduate, they all must meet it. . . .

As shown in Excerpt One, students frequently retake Regents exams, particularly the English Regents. In Excerpt Two, "Ms. V" notes that about 60% of ELLs pass the English Regents at any given time at her school, which means that at least 40% will need to retake the exam to pursue a high school diploma. It is safe to assume that of the 60% of ELLs who passed, a significant number were retaking the exam because they had failed it previously. Retaking is part of exam culture in high schools serving large numbers of ELLs, showing the enormous challenge of the exams and how they define ELL students' experiences in school.

Students and teachers repeatedly refer to the English and Math Regents exams in interviews as the most difficult for ELLs to pass. The statistics that Ms. V shares above are actually far higher than citywide performance by ELLs. In fact, just 33.2% of ELLs passed the English Regents exam in 2005, as compared to a pass rate of 80.7% of all students on the English Regents exam in the same year. For the Math A Regents exam, the ELL citywide pass rate in 2005 was 58.1% as compared to an overall pass rate of 81.5%. . . .

Extended Schooling for ELLs

High school in the United States is typically four years in length, yet this has actually become atypical for ELLs attending school within a high-stakes testing climate. Barring students from high school graduation until they pass the Regents exams has a number of consequences, which include ELLs attending high school for more years, attending more classes per day, and attending more after-school and tutoring programs than native English speakers. The quotations offered above show how students in New York are prevented from graduation because of their test scores, even when they have successfully completed all of their coursework. Similarly, as clarified further in the section that follows, older ELLs are often required to repeat grades of high school they may have completed in their home country to give them a chance at passing the Regents exams; high school counselors at the schools in this study routinely place new arrivals to high school in ninth grade, even when they are overage and have the necessary credits from their home country to place them in a higher grade. As a result, ELLs systematically stay in school beyond the traditional four years. These findings are consistent with nationwide research, as the Center on Education Policy found that the length of time ELLs must attend school has lengthened across the United States due to testing.

Because of the many challenges ELLs must overcome to pass the Regents exams, they are often encouraged or required to attend longer school days than what is required of native English speakers. . . .

City University of New York (CUNY) colleges will accept students who have not passed the Regents exams for admission and allow them to take up to three classes, but will not allow them to actually matriculate until they receive a high school diploma. ESL teachers at School #2 also informed me about students who had been admitted to college but could not graduate or matriculate because of the Regents exams. . . . This means that a single test score will override an institution of higher education's assessment of a student's college readiness.

Testing and the Drop-Out Rate

Of great concern is that because of the challenges that the Regents exams pose for ELLs and their high-stakes consequences, the exams act to push these students to leave school, either of their own volition or with their school's encouragement. The students most likely to leave or be pressured to leave are older ELLs. Students leave school to return to their home country and obtain a high school diploma there, to enter a Graduate

Equivalency Diploma (GED) program in the United States, or to drop out of school completely. In this discussion, it is important to keep in mind that the enrollment of students in most urban high schools in the US decreases dramatically by senior year—a problem which is particularly acute in such cities as Los Angeles, Chicago, New York, Houston and Philadelphia. For instance, the population by grade at the focal school studied in New York City is as follows: 1145 ninth graders, 1154 tenth graders, 730 11th graders, and just 479 12th graders. Seniors . . . who have successfully passed their courses and attained the necessary credits for graduation, are actually high achievers in their grade cohort [statistical group]. Of all the students who started school in freshman year with them, they are among a minority who actually made it so far in high school. Yet these students are being barred from high school graduation because of the Regents exams, which act as a final gatekeeper for the select ELL students to have arrived to the point where they are actually eligible for graduation. Many link low graduation rates to testing:

> Ms. K [an ESL coordinator]: . . . One big effect of the standardized testing is that they're not graduating!!! Very few are actually graduating!! We get six or seven sections of freshmen, and we get three graduating. It's dropping rapidly.

In this excerpt, an ESL coordinator discusses how the Regents exams reduce the graduation rates among ELLs at her school.

In gathering data for the purposes of this research, I learned that the moment an English language learner arrives to a high school in New York City, they are often advised by school guidance counselors or teachers that it will most likely take the student longer than the traditional four years to graduate. If that student is older, they are routinely encouraged to return to the country from which they have just arrived to finish high school. . . .

This is the new reception for ELLs who arrive in the United States during high school; schools are under pressure not to teach those who are hardest to teach, and this limits the opportunities offered to ELLs.

Similarly, older ELL students and others who are struggling in school are often asked to leave school to pursue a GED, even though they have a legal right to remain.

> "Rather than water down the tests, let's invest in intensive language training for the kids still struggling with English."

Standardized Tests Should Be Given in English to ESL Students

Paul Greenberg

Paul Greenberg is a conservative commentator and a syndicated columnist. In the following viewpoint he argues that non–English-speaking students should be given the same tests as everyone else in order to determine their English proficiency. He contends that English is essential to U.S. identity and maintains that allowing students to take tests in their own language is not a good option. Instead, he argues that it should be a priority to make non–English-speaking proficient in English.

As you read, consider the following questions:

1. Why does Greenberg feel that portfolios are not a good way to assess non–English-speakers' educational progress?

2. What does the author fear will happen if the United States attempts to follow Canada's lead in allowing more than one official language?

3. Who is Therese Thompson, and what does Greenberg like about her approach to teaching non–English-speakers?

Question: Why would the U.S. Education Department insist a kid who has little or no English take his year-end tests in English? There are some 4,000 such students in Arkansas alone. Everybody knows they're going to flunk the test. Why make them take it?

Answer: So we'll know who these kids are, where they are, and just how far behind in English they are. That way, we can concentrate on helping them pass the test later.

English Is Vital

Why bother? Because it's important that these youngsters become fluent in the language of their adopted country. Let's not pretend they're being educated (and prepared for citizenship) if they don't know how to read and write English in this one nation indivisible by language.

Here in Arkansas, such students have been allowed to make notebooks—portfolios—to demonstrate their educational progress. But everybody knows, or should know, that putting together a scrapbook is not the same as being fluent in English.

Now that the feds insist these kids be tested, folks complain. But the feds are to be complimented, not badmouthed, when they take this No Child Left Behind [a 2002 federal education reform act] business seriously. And that means not leaving little Jorge or Maria behind, either.

Various alternative ways to test such kids are being explored by the specialists who teach ESL, or English as a Second Language, but none of those ways sound as good as preparing the student to take the test with better results next time. Yes, it's hard. But better to accept a tough challenge than spend all this time and energy devising ways around it.

The worst of these cop-outs is the suggestion the student be given the standardized test in his native language. That's a great way to encourage a bilingual society complete with bilingual tensions. See Canada/Quebec.[1]

Granted, the comparison is not exactly accurate, because our population is even more diverse than Canada's. Go that route and we'll soon have a trilingual, quadrilingual and generally multilingual country, considering how varied the waves of American immigration tend to be. Canada's bilingualism would look simple compared to the patchwork of languages Americans would use if everyone got to take standardized tests in his own native tongue—from Armenian to Zulu.

Train for the Test

I confess that, coming from a Yiddish-speaking home[2], I never had any formal education in mama-loshen, my mother tongue. I had to make do with my immigrant mother helping me piece out the headlines letter-by-letter in the *Forvertz*, the Yiddish paper that showed up in the mailbox every week. I can still hear her reading the tearjerkers in the advice column to my grandmother. (Even then I knew they weren't exactly great literature.)

If only I had been given some Yiddish education, I might now be able to read Sholem Aleichem, the creator of the Tevye stories, as in "Fiddler on the Roof," in the original. Not to mention I.L. Peretz, the brothers Singer [Isaac Bashevis and Israel Joshua], and, well, a whole literature and therefore world. Yiddish may be a small, even diminutive, language, but there are those who love it.

---

1. Canada is a bilingual society, utilizing both French and English officially. Quebec, which has more French speakers than other parts of Canada, has threatened to secede on several occasions.
2. Yiddish is a language spoken by Eastern European Jews.

Still, I'm grateful that, once I entered public school, it was conducted in English, including the tests. The monolingual may not believe it, but it seemed perfectly natural to switch from Yiddish at home to English in school and go on to Hebrew School in the afternoons.

A child's sponge-like mind can do that. Kids in Spanish-speaking homes all over the country are probably changing languages just as naturally today whenever they walk in and out the door.

Rather than water down the tests, let's invest in intensive language training for the kids still struggling with English, whether they're Chinese in San Francisco, Cajun in South Louisiana, Portuguese in Boston—or Hispanic in Arkansas.

Because they're all American, and one can scarcely be American without knowing English, or what passes for it on this side of the Atlantic—whether the dialect is Maine Yankee or Arkinsaw Suthuhn.

What's the best approach to take toward kids without much English?

Well, I've been reading about a fifth-grader at the John Tyson Elementary School in Springdale, Ark. His literacy instructor, Therese Thompson, isn't about to wait the estimated two years it would take for the ESL establishment to come up with alternatives to the regular tests. She notes that the state's next standardized exams will be given in April: "We've got all of December, January, February and March to get him there."

That's the spirit. What's needed is not non-English tests, or tests that use "simplified" English but more Therese Thompsons.

Periodical Bibliography

The following articles have been selected to supplement the diverse views presented in this chapter.

William J. Bennett and Rod Paige	"Why We Need a National Test," *Washington Post*, September 21, 2006.
Bronwyn Coltrane	"English Language Learners and High-Stakes Tests: An Overview of the Issues," Center for Applied Linguistics, November 2002. www.cal.org.
Greg Fish	"Stop the Standardized Test Tyranny," *BusinessWeek*, February 2009.
Dan Fletcher	"A Brief History of Standardized Testing," *Time*, December 11, 2009.
Dana Goldstein	"Testing Testing," *American Prospect*, July 2, 2009.
Jay P. Greene and Marcus Winters	"High-Stakes Editorializing," *National Review Online*, February 23, 2004. http://article.nationalreview.com.
Jennifer Luo	"CSAP Can Sharpen Test Takers," *Denver Post*, October 14, 2007. www.denverpost.com.
Jay Matthews	"Just Whose Idea Was All This Testing?" *Washington Post*, November 11, 2006.
Richard Rothstein	"Too Young to Test," *American Prospect*, November 1, 2004.
Michael Winerip	"Standardized Tests Face a Crisis in Standards," *New York Times*, March 22, 2006.

CHAPTER 3

What Role Should Testing Play in Evaluating Teachers and Schools?

Chapter Preface

The official goal of Chicago Public Schools' Renaissance 2010 initiative was to "increase the number of high quality educational options in communities across Chicago by 2010," according to the Renaissance 2010 Web site. The schools were to be established through a "competitive, community-based selection process," and all schools were to be held accountable to given standards. The program was especially interested in promoting charter schools, which would have more flexibility than traditional public schools but would be required to adhere to a particular charter, or plan. Renaissance 2010 hoped to open one hundred schools by the end of 2010.

While it was meant to open schools, however, many fear that Renaissance 2010 has mainly done the opposite. Linda Lutton in a January 12, 2010, report on Chicago Public Radio noted that Renaissance 2010 had come to be seen by many as a program to close schools down rather than to start them up. Lutton reported that Chicago Public Schools had shut down fifty-six schools and fired the staff at eleven others since the beginning of Renaissance 2010. Activists opposed to these school closings argued that Renaissance 2010 was actually hurting rather than helping neighborhood schools.

In January 2010, a number of Chicago schools were targeted for closure or academic turnaround because of poor performance on state tests. Marshall, one of the schools targeted for turnaround, had fallen from 15 percent of students passing state tests in 2006 to only 3.9 percent passing in 2009, according to a January 19, 2010, report on the WBBM News Radio Web site.

Despite such dismal performances, however, parents, teachers, and students protested the dramatic changes. Speaking at the Chicago Board of Education's monthly meeting, Jennifer Kush, a high school sophomore, said that students should not be shipped from one school to another "like we are not worth working with." Kush also expressed concern that closing schools increases violence when gang members from one area are forced to start attending a school in a different neighborhood. Other protesters worried that severing relationships between students and teachers would not improve education, according to a January 27, 2010, article on the Chicago Breaking News Center Web site.

The struggle over Renaissance 2010 demonstrates the ongoing controversy around using test scores to make decisions about the fate of schools, teachers, and students. In the following viewpoints, writers discuss these difficulties from a number of other perspectives.

> "There's no reason why teachers shouldn't ... be evaluated against objective measures of student performance."

Student Test Scores Should Be Part of Teacher Evaluation

Camille Esch

Camille Esch is an Irvine fellow at the New America Foundation, specializing in education policy. In the following viewpoint, she argues that current teacher evaluations are too subjective and lenient. She says that student test scores should be used to provide better evidence of teacher competence. Esch adds that tests should be only one form of evaluation. She also notes that care must be taken to develop new tests that accurately judge teachers without unfairly penalizing those in low-performing schools.

As you read, consider the following questions:

1. According to Esch, how are teachers evaluated in most school districts?

2. What methods does the author suggest might be used to evaluate teachers in addition to student test scores?

3. What problems does Esch identify with using existing assessment tests to measure teacher performance?

In recent years, reformers have sought to improve our failing public education system by tightening and standardizing the measures we use to judge performance. From the numerical requirements of the No Child Left Behind Act [a federal education reform law passed in 2001] to California's increased focus on assessment and accountability, there's been a conscious attempt to use hard data to measure success at every level of the education system.

More Objective Evaluations

But one group does not have its performance measured this way: teachers. Determining the effectiveness of individual teachers—are they helping our kids learn or not?—remains a mostly subjective judgment. Yet there's no reason why teachers shouldn't also be evaluated against objective measures of student performance just as are schools, districts and states.

Teacher evaluations focus on what they do in the classroom—the input of the learning process. In most school districts, principals show up at prearranged times to observe teachers' work, and then write their observations. In doing this, they typically use a checklist to guide their assessments. Evaluations usually consist of one or two written observations.

This superficial and largely subjective approach to evaluating teachers is something of a farce. In many instances, principals can only rate teachers "satisfactory" or "unsatisfactory." Multiple unsatisfactory evaluations can lead to dismissal. But faced with the prospect of battling the local teachers union to prove that a teacher's unsatisfactory evaluation is valid, most principals capitulate and rate virtually all teachers as satisfactory.

This rubber-stamp routine may make things easier for administrators, but not for the kids. Several researchers, among them Eric Hanushek of the Hoover Institution of Stanford University and Jonah Rockoff of Columbia University, have shown that teachers are not interchangeable when it comes to student learning. Given a year with an effective teacher—one whose pupils previously showed test-score gains—students can advance their learning by a grade level or more, according to research done by William L. Sanders while he was at the University of Tennessee. He also found that under a weak teacher, kids' progress can stall, and they can fall behind.

So why not include student test scores—the output of the learning process—in teachers' evaluations? Besides giving the evaluation process a much needed shot of objectivity and rigor, this change could help administrators target assistance for struggling teachers and recognize those who are most effective in the classroom.

Test Scores Can Help Evaluations

In its report [in March 2008], [California] Gov. Arnold Schwarzenegger's nonpartisan committee of education experts agreed. Among other things, it recommended that teacher evaluations should be based in part on student achievement.

Teachers unions object to using student test scores to evaluate teachers. They argue that these scores are influenced by many factors beyond a teacher's control—students' home environments, language abilities, whether they ate breakfast on the morning of a test. True enough, but this is not a reason to ignore student achievement altogether.

Of course, student test-score data should not be the sole measure of a teacher's performance. It should be combined with other factors to produce a well-rounded assessment, including more rigorous and more frequent classroom observations by principals, announced and unannounced, as well as reviews of teachers' lesson plans and homework assignments by principals or peers.

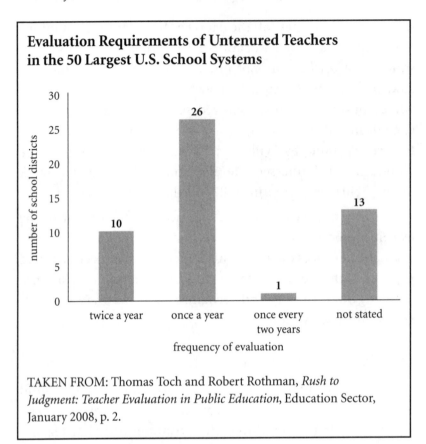

Evaluation Requirements of Untenured Teachers in the 50 Largest U.S. School Systems

TAKEN FROM: Thomas Toch and Robert Rothman, *Rush to Judgment: Teacher Evaluation in Public Education*, Education Sector, January 2008, p. 2.

And incorporating students' test data into teachers' evaluations should be done in a way that ensures fairness. For starters, not just absolute student test performance should be taken into account, but also how much students grow over the course of a year. For instance, a teacher could make phenomenal progress with struggling students but still not get them to a high achievement. In this case, the teacher should be rewarded, not penalized. This approach would prevent teachers from fleeing low-performing schools or classes.

Second, evaluation must consider extenuating circumstances. For instance, if a first-year English teacher is assigned to teach chemistry, he shouldn't be blamed for less-than-stellar test scores.

Finally, any attempt to use test scores to help evaluate teachers should not be done on the cheap. Policymakers may be tempted to co-opt existing assessments like California's STAR tests [which measure student mastery on the basis of state academic content standards] for the purposes of teacher evaluation. But these standardized tests are designed to give information about how a school, district or state is performing, and they don't cover all subject areas. To build a better system of evaluating teachers, it is worth the investment to design tests that measure how much individual students learn over the course of a year on the material the teacher is expected to teach.

There's no question that teachers have tough jobs. But the old evaluation system that ignores student achievement and finds virtually all teachers "satisfactory" simply sets the bar too low, lacks objectivity and does not address whether students are actually learning. If we want to give students the best chance at success, we need to do a better job of determining whether their teachers are helping them. Evaluating teachers with no hard evidence about their primary responsibility is just plain irresponsible.

| *"Experts ... have argued that state tests are not designed for teacher evaluation and will not yield reliable results."*

Teachers Should Not Be Evaluated Using Student Test Scores

David B. Cohen and Alex Kajitani

David B. Cohen teaches ninth and tenth-grade English at Palo Alto High School in Palo Alto, California. Alex Kajitani teaches eighth-grade algebra at Mission Middle School in Escondido, California. In the following viewpoint, they argue that student tests are not designed to be used to evaluate teacher performance. Instead, they claim, tests of math and reading evaluate only limited skills and emphasize testing over real learning. They conclude that emphasizing testing hurts students, and they urge the use of other methods to evaluate teacher performance.

As you read, consider the following questions:

1. At what sort of schools do Cohen and Kajitani work?

David B. Cohen and Alex Kajitani, "Test Scores Poor Tool for Teacher Evaluation," *Sacramento Bee*, September 3, 2009. Copyright © 2009 The Sacramento Bee. Reproduced by permission.

2. According to the authors, what skills must Kajitani focus on instead of conceptual reasoning because of state tests?

3. What do Cohen and Kajitani recommend as an alternative means of student and teacher evaluations?

Education Secretary Arne Duncan is in Sacramento [California] today [in September 2009] to promote the Race to the Top grant program, which offers a chunk of $4.5 billion in federal funds to states that meet federal guidelines, including a requirement to allow standardized test results to be used in individual teacher evaluations.

Evaluations Will Not Work

The link between test scores and teacher performance may seem obvious to the casual observer, but this is a case where appearances and intuition are misleading. As two of California's teachers—the 2009 California Teacher of the Year and a National Board-certified teacher—we urge Duncan and [California] Gov. Arnold Schwarzenegger to go back to school regarding the use of test scores for teacher evaluations.

Currently, state education policy prohibits this practice; experts in education, testing and even economics have argued that state tests are not designed for teacher evaluation and will not yield reliable results. You are taking us in a direction that will harm our schools and our students.

The policy changes promoted through Race to the Top will undo California's thoughtful, research-based and consensus-driven state education policy in an attempt to qualify for federal grants. But after we have exchanged good policy for bad in pursuit of short-term funding, what will we do when the money runs out? We will be stuck with a hastily changed state policy that exacerbates the exact problems that made No Child Left Behind [the 2002 federal education policy begun by the George W. Bush administration] a failed initiative.

Tests Evaluate Only Basic Skills

One school of reformers . . . would evaluate teachers on the basis of their students' achievement. It's a reasonable strategy: It's the most direct way to measure teacher performance, and teaching is ultimately about helping students learn. But currently the only way to measure student achievement on a large scale is with standardized test scores. And that makes the student-achievement strategy difficult.

For one thing, only about half the nation's teachers teach subjects that are tested. It wouldn't be possible to use student test scores in individual teacher evaluations for the other half.

Secondly, a majority of the standardized tests that would be used in teacher evaluations today . . . focus on low-level skills such as the recall or restatement of information and on only a few subjects, primarily reading, math, and science. They don't measure more advanced skills such as expository writing or an ability to think creatively or analytically, and they sidestep history, art, music, and other subjects. . . . It might be reasonable, as a result, to use test scores as a factor in weeding out the weakest teachers, but they wouldn't be as good at identifying the best teachers.

> *Thomas Toch and Robert Rothman,*
> Rush to Judgment:
> Teacher Evaluation in Public Education,
> *January 2008. www.educationsector.org.*

The overemphasis on testing does not enhance educational quality, but instead will promote schooling that leaves too many of our children underprepared for higher education, unskilled at critical thinking and less engaged in their communities. Parents and business leaders consistently say they want us to develop in students the types of skills least valued in a test-driven educational atmosphere.

Now, we are not teachers who are afraid of evaluation, or who are trying to protect our jobs. We have both been evaluated rigorously to reach the positions we are in, and we welcome deep and detailed evaluation because it elevates our teaching. Our schools are quite different. (David Cohen works in an affluent community at a high-performing suburban high school, and Alex Kajitani works in a low-performing middle school in one of Southern California's most poverty-stricken neighborhoods.) Neither of us believes that standardized test scores accurately illustrate our students' learning or our abilities as teachers.

Testing the Wrong Skills

Like English teachers across California, Cohen works with a set of standards requiring instruction in a range of language arts skills: reading, writing, listening and speaking. Two of these four standards areas are entirely ignored by state tests that offer no listening or speaking components. The tests mostly measure writing skills by checking some basic proofreading skills, but usually, no actual writing.

The all-important reading assessments are similarly narrow and are further suspect because test-savvy students work backward from the questions and don't have to read the passages, and then rely on a variety of outside knowledge to eliminate obvious wrong answers; meanwhile, test-averse students often post scores masking their true abilities. How then can the practice of an English teacher be accurately measured with tests that hardly overlap with the teaching expected of us?

Kajitani, a math teacher, knows that before each test period it is time to pause the teaching of true problem-solving and conceptual reasoning to be sure that students have memorized the operations on which they will be tested and to refresh their test-taking skills. Effective teachers may know how to squeeze in both "teaching to the test" and teaching real, in-depth critical thinking, but this begs the question of where the teacher's time is best spent, for the true benefit of the children they are educating. We sacrifice better learning for better test scores.

Most state tests yield results that are valuable to teachers if we want to know only how students perform on the tests. When we want to know more about our students and their full range of skills and knowledge, the tests mean very little. Respect for our students and respect for our teaching both demand evaluation based on a broad range of information and multiple measures of performance. Test-driven policies notoriously push in the opposite direction.

Our current education code makes clear that test scores and teacher data are to be used to evaluate systems and programs, not individual teachers. As members of the Accomplished California Teachers network [established by Stanford University to connect teachers and policy makers], we support efforts to create more effective evaluations, with greater focus on actual teaching practices, including robust and varied evidence such as student and teacher portfolios. But evaluating individual teachers based on test scores, in a reactionary effort to complete for Race to the Top money, is not the answer. It would be a travesty of education reform for the teachers and students of our state.

> "The only way to evaluate a teacher-training program is to look at how the teachers perform once in the classroom; the only way to do that is to measure how the students are doing."

Teacher-Training Program Evaluation Should Be Based on Student Test Scores

Ruben Navarrette

Ruben Navarrette is a member of the editorial board of the San Diego (CA) Union-Tribune *and a nationally syndicated columnist. In the following viewpoint, he argues that teacher training is poor and does not prepare teachers for the classroom. He suggests that training would improve if it were linked to student performance, so that those who teach teachers could be held accountable for the success or failure of the teachers' students.*

As you read, consider the following questions:

1. According to Navarrette, what groups of students do those who teach in schools of education not know how to reach?

2. How does Louisiana link student achievement with teacher education, according to the author?

3. Why does Navarrette believe that it is easy to hide bad teaching and mediocre training?

By stalling on issues ranging from Afghanistan to immigration reform, President Barack Obama has earned a reputation for being indecisive. Yet Obama did make one decision that was positively brilliant—naming Arne Duncan as secretary of education.

Mediocre Teachers Colleges

Duncan proved this again [in October 2009] when he zeroed in on an often-overlooked part of the education reform equation: the nation's teachers colleges. In a speech at Columbia University's Teachers College, Duncan delivered a stinging critique of the schools that trained most of the more than 3 million teachers who currently work in U.S. public schools.

"By almost any standard," Duncan told an audience of student teachers and faculty, "many if not most of the nation's 1,450 schools, colleges and departments of education are doing a mediocre job of preparing teachers for the realities of the 21st-century classroom."

The word "mediocre" had extra bite because teachers colleges are, as *Time* magazine put it, "the stepchildren of the American university system."

Duncan is onto something. With so much scrutiny aimed at measuring student performance from kindergarten through high school, many education reformers never get around to asking embarrassing questions about how well teachers are doing in their profession, where they got their training, how much they learned, and what can be improved. Until we start scrutinizing this part of the process, and look at who is teaching the teachers, we'll never empower students to reach their academic potential and create a work force that is globally competitive.

Most of the criticism I hear about teachers colleges—from education professors, student teachers and teachers in the classroom—centers around the idea that teachers are being shortchanged. Critics say that the training teachers are getting is 20 years behind the times and that it is too heavily steeped in theory and not useful in the real world of the classroom. They say that those who teach in schools of education are clueless about how to reach children with dyslexia, attention deficit disorder, Asperger's syndrome or other learning challenges. Lastly, they say, there is no tolerance for dissenting views and that once a professor states an opinion about anything from standardized testing to bilingual education and selects the research to back it up, students are expected to fall in line.

Evaluated on Student Outcomes

Duncan must be hearing the same sort of criticisms. He understands that the only way to evaluate a teacher-training program is to look at how the teachers perform once in the classroom; the only way to do that is to measure how the students are doing. It's all connected.

"I am urging every teacher-education program today to make better outcomes for students the overarching mission that propels every single one of their efforts," he said.

Duncan especially likes what Louisiana did as part of the rebuilding effort after Hurricane Katrina [which devastated the city of New Orleans in 2005]. The state takes student test scores in grades 4–9 and traces them back to their teachers, who are then traced back to whatever institution gave them their training and certification. The state shares that information with the schools of education, and urges the schools to improve. Duncan wants other states to follow suit, and he's dangling part of a $4.35 billion fund under the [Obama] administration's Race to the Top initiative, [begun in 2009] whose emphasis on standards and accountability bears a striking resemblance to the [George W.] Bush administration's [2002] education reform law—No Child Left Behind.

The "trace back" is groundbreaking stuff. Imagine tracking students back to teachers, and tracing teachers back to schools of education. Now that's accountability. It is no wonder that concept always scares the daylights out of some people. For all the complaints that teachers have—about parents, students, administrators, salaries, testing, budget cuts, etc.—there is one thing that still makes it a great job for those who don't like taking responsibility or accepting blame: anonymity.

When students graduate from high school, whether it's at the top of the class or at the bottom, they may have had dozens of teachers since kindergarten. All of those teachers, it could be argued, are at least partly responsible for a student's academic success or failure.

So it's easy to hide bad teaching and mediocre training, which only ensures we'll get more of both. As it stands, it's also easy for principals and superintendents to give lip service to the idea that the entire system is responsible for how well students perform.

And when everyone is responsible, no one is responsible.

> *"We lack empirical evidence of what works in preparing teachers for an outcome-based education system."*

Teacher-Training Program Evaluation Cannot Be Based on Student Test Scores

Arthur Levine

Arthur Levine is the president of the Woodrow Wilson Foundation and former president and professor of education at Teachers College, Columbia University. In the following viewpoint, he asserts that approaches to teacher education are extremely controversial. Some argue that teaching should be professionalized and taught from universities, whereas others argue it should be treated as a craft and taught through alternative routes. Levine contends, however, that these debates are based on little real evidence, as little research has been done to relate teacher education to student achievement.

As you read, consider the following questions:

1. On what basis did education secretary Rod Paige believe teachers should be hired, according to the author?

2. According to Levine, what types of teachers, school systems, or students are more likely to be taught by teachers prepared for a craft?

3. Process-based school systems assess education success in what ways, according to the author?

There is a schism over the how's and when's of teacher education between those who believe teaching is a profession like law or medicine, requiring a substantial amount of education before an individual can become a practitioner, and those who think teaching is a craft like journalism, which is learned principally on the job.

How Should Teachers Be Educated?

This debate drew national attention in 2002 when U.S. Secretary of Education Rod Paige, a former school superintendent and education school dean, embraced the craft position. In his annual report that year, he wrote that there "was little evidence that education school course work leads to improved student achievement." He drew this conclusion from a study by the Abell Foundation, entitled *Teacher Certification Reconsidered: Stumbling for Quality,* This study characterized 50 years of teacher education research as "flawed, sloppy, aged, and sometimes academically dishonest." Like the foundation, Paige recommended that teachers be hired on the basis of their subject matter knowledge and verbal ability; education school course work should be made optional and student teaching should be eliminated as a requirement for new teachers.

Those who believed teaching is a profession responded loudly, stating that rigorous preparation was essential to educating teachers. They said reductions in pre-service course work in education would diminish student learning in schools, increase teacher attrition, and disproportionately affect the most disadvantaged children in America. The same half-century of studies dismissed by Abell were offered in evidence. The work of the Abell Foundation was criticized for being "littered with inaccuracies, misstatements, and misrepresentations."

The Abell Foundation replied in kind. In the words of the trade newspaper *Education Week*, the exchange was a battle royale—"the charges flew like chairs on *The Jerry Springer Show*." Using words like 'shameful' and 'dishonest,' the parties accused each other of hypocrisy and of harboring ulterior motives."

This was no ordinary clash. Try to imagine the same thing happening in medicine. It is difficult to conceive of a debate over whether medical school study by physicians improves patient health. Would national health care be enhanced if physician licensure were awarded to people with subject mastery of the basic sciences and high verbal ability and if study in medical school were made optional?

But the debate did occur in teacher education. Today, both sides view their positions as matters of faith; the rhetoric is white hot; and there is no room for compromise. The clash of beliefs is reshaping the world of teacher education, driving it headlong in opposing and incompatible directions.

More Regulation or Less?

On one hand, reflecting the position that teaching is a profession, states have created a more regulated and regimented environment that strives to improve teacher quality, demands higher standards of the people entering the teaching profession, and seeks greater accountability from teachers and the institutions that prepare them.

Integral to this has been increased teacher testing for certification in the areas of basic skills, subject matter, and pedagogy. The states have also adopted accountability measures for education schools, including the publication of institutional pass rates for graduates on teacher licensing exams, identification of low-performing schools of education, and experimentation with accountability based on student achievement in classes taught by alumni.

On the other hand, the belief that teaching is a craft, compounded by pressure to find enough teachers to fill empty [teaching positions], has resulted in many states' deregulating entry requirements for teachers, creating a more open marketplace for teacher education. There is now greater variability in what is required to enter teaching, multiplication in the number of pathways into teaching, and a diminished role for university-based teacher education programs. Today 47 states and the District of Columbia have adopted alternative route programs, designed to speed entry of teachers into the classroom and reduce or eliminate education school course work. In the past quarter-century, they have permitted more than a quarter million people to earn teaching credentials, most within the past decade.

The rise of divergent routes into the classroom has been accelerated by the federal government. The No Child Left Behind (NCLB) law [of 2002] defines "highly qualified" teachers as persons with subject matter mastery, but without traditional university-based teacher education classes.

The bottom line is that the U.S. lacks a common vision of how to prepare teachers to meet today's new realities, leading to the rise of divergent and opposing approaches to reform.

Where Should Teachers Be Educated?

The profession/craft debate also raises the question of where teachers should be educated: in traditional university-based programs or via an expanding number of non-university alternative route programs, which tend to be mirror images of one another? The traditional programs, relying on professors as their primary faculty, can be characterized as more theoretical and academic, while the non-university programs, utilizing practitioners as their principal instructors, emphasize practice and field work. The course of studies is also longer in university programs, reflecting differences in the amount of preparation believed necessary to enter a classroom.

For those preparing for a profession, pre-service teacher education generally takes place in one of nearly 1,200 colleges and universities, found at 78 percent of the nation's four-year schools. In 2002–03, these programs produced almost 106,000 teacher education baccalaureate degrees, more than 64,000 master's degrees, nearly 1,000 doctoral degrees, and over 4,000 certificates in teacher education.

The greatest commonality among university-based teacher education programs is their diversity. The institutions housing them vary from open admission baccalaureate-granting colleges to the most selective doctoral-awarding universities. The programs educate teachers at the undergraduate and graduate levels. They award baccalaureate degrees, master's degrees, and certificates. They may require majors in education, majors in the liberal arts, majors in the liberal arts and education, and minors in teacher education or the liberal arts.

Alternative Programs

Those being prepared for a craft reach the classroom through an equally diverse array of programs, offered under the banner of alternative routes to teacher certification, a term referring to a collection of programs linked more by what they *are not* than what they are.

They are everything under the sun except traditional university teacher preparation programs. Emily Feistritzer, president of the National Center for Education Information, has studied a variety of alternative programs around the country. She has reported wide variation in program content. While 90 percent of the participants teach full time during their studies, only 61 percent take college education courses. If they do take courses, the number of credits ranges from fewer than six (14 percent) to more than 41 (8 percent). The median range is 13 to 18 credits.

The staffing of the programs follows the same pattern. Most commonly, students work with mentor teachers (90 percent) and school district staff members (85 percent). Less frequently, they study with professors on college campuses (54 percent) and college faculty members in their schools (36 percent).

The providers of non-collegiate teacher education run the gamut from for-profit companies such as the education school of the online Kaplan University (owned by the *Washington Post*) to non-profits such as Teach for America; from community colleges to school systems; and from regional education services to individual public schools. Their numbers are booming.

In conclusion, the divergences in belief regarding where teachers should be prepared once again leads to conflicting and inconsistent directions for improving teacher education. We are divided about whether the primary faculty should be academics or practitioners. We disagree about whether the curriculum should be largely course work or field experience. And, of course, we differ regarding the amount of education students require before entering the classroom. The enormous diversity of practices within university and non-university teacher education muddles the path further.

What makes this situation especially troubling is the likelihood of systematic differences in how teachers are educated for differing types of schools, subjects, and students. For instance, it seems that teachers in urban schools would more likely be prepared for a craft than their counterparts in suburban schools. Hard-to-staff subjects would also be more likely to employ teachers educated via alternative routes. Low-income children of color would more likely be taught by teachers educated for a craft than their more affluent white peers. School systems concerned principally with increasing the number of teachers would be more likely to hire faculty prepared for a craft, while school systems emphasizing qualitative improvement would more likely be inclined to recruit teachers prepared for a profession. In short, teachers are likely to be taking dramatically different courses of study to prepare to teach in the same school districts.

A Shift in Focus

The divides over whether teaching is a profession or a career, whether teacher education should be the province of schools of education or alternative providers, and whether teachers should learn their jobs before entering a classroom or in the classroom while on the job, are exacerbated by the changing expectations for P[reschool]–12 schools. The shift in focus from common processes for all schools to common outcomes for all children changes the measure of success for teachers. Process-based school systems, rooted in what students are taught, assesses education success in terms of issues such as teacher knowledge and credentials, curriculum design and organization, and reliable and valid assessment methods. In contrast, outcome-based systems, concerned with what students learn, have a single measure of success—student achievement.

Therein lies the problem. The voluminous body of research on teaching was produced largely before the shift to common outcomes. As a result, we don't know enough about the impact of teacher education on student achievement. We do not know whether university-based or non-university-based teacher education is superior. We don't know whether educating teachers for a profession or a craft is more effective in raising student achievement.

Study after study has reported limitations in the existing research. With regard to university-based teacher education, a Michigan State University meta-study found: "There is no research that directly assesses what teachers learn in their peda-

The Three Most Important Proposals for Improving Teacher Preparation

Principals, education school alumni, faculty, and deans weighed in on what they perceived to be the three most important steps to ensure teacher preparedness.

Proposal	Percent selecting			
	Principals	Alumni	Faculty	Deans
Strike a better balance between subject matter preparation and field experience	57%	69%	49%	13%
Require student teaching of longer duration	31%	26%	22%	23%
Provide closer supervision of student teaching	18%	21%	21%	21%
Divide professors into clinical and research categories	6%	14%	16%	13%
Mentor new teachers	50%	63%	69%	70%
Require a major in an academic subject other than education at the undergraduate level	17%	27%	34%	24%
Increase mastery of pedagogical practice	26%	27%	41%	43%
Raise requirements for academic performance	7%	14%	23%	17%
Recruit higher quality faculty	7%	16%	13%	8%

TAKEN FROM: Arthur Levine, *Educating School Teachers*, The Education School Project, September 2006, p. 38.

gogical preparation and then evaluates the relationship of that pedagogical knowledge to student learning or teacher behavior." There is also "no research that directly assesses prospective teachers' subject matter knowledge and then evaluates the relationship between teacher subject matter preparation and student learning."

Unfortunately, critics of university-based teacher education often treat the absence of research as a negative finding. That is, instead of concluding that we don't yet know about the impact of university-based teacher education on student classroom achievement, they have acted as if the absence of research is the equivalent of finding that the university-based programs have at best no impact or may actually reduce student achievement. This has fueled the expansion of alternative routes and encouraged alternative providers.

The state of research on the efficacy of alternative route programs is no better. Few studies exist, and most of those rely on satisfaction surveys and a basketful of anecdotes. Indeed, [Kenneth M.] Zeichner and [Hilary G.] Conklin carried out a meta-study of the peer-reviewed empirical research comparing traditional and alternative route programs. They compared both approaches in a variety of settings and reported serious methodological flaws in the research, very little difference in the outcomes, and inconclusive findings.

The bottom line is that we lack empirical evidence of what works in preparing teachers for an outcome-based education system. We don't know what, where, how, or when teacher education is most effective. This means the education our teachers receive today is determined more by ideology and personal predilection than the needs of our children.

"When conscientiously applied strategies fail to drastically improve America's lowest-performing schools, we need to close them."

Failing Schools Should Be Closed

Andy Smarick

Andy Smarick is a distinguished visiting fellow at the Thomas B. Fordham Institute and adjunct fellow at the American Enterprise Institute. In the following viewpoint, he argues that turning around failing schools is extremely difficult and that despite much experimentation, no successful and reliable procedure for doing so has been developed. Rather than continuing to try to improve failing schools, therefore, he suggests closing such schools and starting new ones based on the charter school model. He asserts that cities like Chicago and New York have already had success with this method and that it could solve many of the problems of the U.S. education system.

As you read, consider the following questions:

1. According to Smarick, what was the result when California targeted its lowest-performing 20 percent of schools for intervention?

2. As cited by the author, what did secretary of education Arne Duncan say the United States could do to change the lives of tens of millions of underserved children?

3. What does Smarick believe are the benefits of "churn"?

For as long as there have been struggling schools in America's cities, there have been efforts to turn them around. . . .

But overall, school turnaround efforts have consistently fallen far short of hopes and expectations. Quite simply, turnarounds are not a scalable strategy for fixing America's troubled urban school systems.

Fortunately, findings from two generations of school improvement efforts, lessons from similar work in other industries, and a budding practice among reform-minded superintendents are pointing to a promising alternative. When conscientiously applied strategies fail to drastically improve America's lowest-performing schools, we need to close them.

Done right, not only will this strategy help the students assigned to these failing schools, it will also have a cascading effect on other policies and practices, ultimately helping to bring about healthy systems of urban public schools.

Very Difficult to Change

Looking back on the history of school turnaround efforts, the first and most important lesson is the "Law of Incessant Inertia." Once persistently low performing, the majority of schools will remain low performing despite being acted upon in innumerable ways.

Examples abound: In the first year of California's Academic Performance Index, the state targeted its lowest-performing 20 percent of schools for intervention. After three years, only 11 percent of the elementary schools in this category (109 of 968) were able to make "exemplary progress." Only 1 of the 394 middle and high schools in this category reached this mark. Just one-quarter of the schools were even able to accomplish a lesser goal: meeting schoolwide and subgroup growth targets each year.

In 2008, 52 Ohio schools were forced to restructure because of persistent failure. Even after several years of significant attention, fewer than one in three had been able to reach established academic goals, and less than half showed any student performance gains. The *Columbus Dispatch* concluded, "Few of them have improved significantly even after years of effort and millions in tax dollars." ...

Though alarming, the poor record for school turnarounds in recent years should come as no surprise. A study published in 2005 by the Education Commission of the States (ECS) on state takeovers of schools and districts noted that the takeovers "have yet to produce dramatic consistent increases in student performance," and that the impact on learning "falls short of expectations."

Reflecting on the wide array of efforts to improve failing schools, one set of analysts concluded, "Turnaround efforts have for the most part resulted in only marginal improvements. . . . Promising practices have failed to work at scale when imported to troubled schools."

Ongoing Ignorance

The second important lesson is the "Law of Ongoing Ignorance." Despite years of experience and great expenditures of time, money, and energy, we still lack basic information about which tactics will make a struggling school excellent. A review published in January 2003 by the Thomas B. Fordham Foundation of more than 100 books, articles, and briefs on turnaround efforts concluded, "There is, at present, no strong evidence that any particular intervention type works most of the time or in most places."

An EdSource study that sought to compare California's low-performing schools that failed to make progress to its low-performing schools that did improve came to a confounding conclusion: clear differences avoided detection. Comparing the two groups, the authors noted, "These were schools in the same cities and districts, often serving children from the same backgrounds. Some of them also adopted the same curriculum programs, had teachers with similar backgrounds, and had similar opportunities for professional development."

Maryland's veteran state superintendent of schools, Nancy Grasmick, agrees: "Very little research exists on how to bring about real sea change in schools. . . . Clearly, there's no infallible strategy or even sequence of them." Responding to the growing number of failing Baltimore schools requiring state-approved improvement plans, she said, "No one has the answer. It's like finding the cure for cancer." . . .

The prevailing view is that we must keep looking for turnaround solutions. Observers have written, "Turnaround at scale is still in its infancy," and, "In education, turnarounds have been tried rarely." But, in fact, the number and scope of fix-it efforts have been extensive to say the least.

Long before NCLB [No Child Left Behind—a 2002 federal school-reform law] required interventions in the lowest-performing schools, states had undertaken significant activity. In 1989 New Jersey took over Jersey City Public Schools; in 1995 it took over Newark Public Schools. In 1993 California took control of the Compton Unified School District. In 1995 Ohio took over the Cleveland Metropolitan School District. Between 1993 and 1997 states required the reconstitution of failing schools in Denver, Chicago, New York City, and Houston. In 2000 Alabama took over a number of schools across the state, and Maryland seized control of three schools in Baltimore.

Since NCLB, interventions in struggling schools have only grown in number and intensity. In the 2006–07 school year, more than 750 schools in "corrective action," the NCLB phase preceding restructuring, implemented a new research-based curriculum, more than 700 used an outside expert to advise the school, nearly 400 restructured the internal organization of the school, and more than 200 extended the school day or year. Importantly, more than 300 replaced staff members or the principal, among the toughest traditional interventions possible.

Occasionally a program will report encouraging success rates. The University of Virginia School Turnaround Specialist Program asserts that about half of its targeted schools have either made AYP [adequate yearly progress, a statewide accountability system] or reduced math and reading failure rates by at least 5 percent. Though this might be better than would otherwise be expected, the threshold for success is remarkably low. It is also unknown whether such progress can be sustained. This matter is particularly important, given that some point to charter management organizations Green Dot and Mastery as turnaround success stories even though each has a very short turnaround résumé, in both numbers of schools and years of experience.

Many schools that reach NCLB's restructuring phase, rather than implementing one of the law's stated interventions (close and reopen as a charter school,[1] replace staff, turn the school over to the state, or contract with an outside entity), choose the "other" option, under which they have consider-

1. Charter schools receive public money, but have different programs and accountability than most public schools. Students generally apply for or choose to attend charter schools.

able flexibility to design an improvement strategy of their own.... Some call this a "loophole" for avoiding tough action.

Yet even under the maligned "other" option, states and districts have tried an astonishing array of improvement strategies, including different types of school-level needs assessments, surveys of school staff, conferences, professional development, turnaround specialists, school improvement committees, training sessions, principal mentors, teacher coaches, leadership facilitators, instructional trainers, subject-matter experts, audits, summer residential academies, student tutoring, research-based reform models, reconfigured grade spans, alternative governance models, new curricula, improved use of data, and turning over operation of some schools to outside organizations.

It's simply impossible to make the case that turnaround efforts haven't been tried or given a chance to work....

More Effort Will Not Help

The [Barack] Obama administration, too, has bought into the notion that turnarounds are the key to improving urban districts. Education secretary Arne Duncan has said that if the nation could turn around 1,000 schools annually for five years, "We could really move the needle, lift the bottom and change the lives of tens of millions of underserved children." In the administration's 2009 stimulus legislation, $3 billion in new funds were appropriated for School Improvement Grants, which aid schools in NCLB improvement status. The administration requested an additional $1.5 billion for this program in the 2010 budget. This is all on top of the numerous streams of existing federal funds that can be—and have been—used to turn around failing schools.

The dissonance is deafening. The history of urban education tells us emphatically that turnarounds are not a reliable strategy for improving our very worst schools. So why does there remain a stubborn insistence on preserving fix-it efforts? . . .

Education leaders seem to believe that, outside of the world of schools, persistent failures are easily fixed. Far from it. The limited success of turnarounds is a common theme in other fields. Writing in *Public Money & Management*, researchers familiar with the true private-sector track record offered a word of caution: "There is a risk that politicians, government officials, and others, newly enamored of the language of failure and turnaround and inadequately informed of the empirical evidence and practical experience in the for-profit sector . . . will have unrealistic expectations of the transformative power of the turnaround process."

[Frederick] Hess and [Thomas] Gift reviewed the success rates of Total Quality Management (TQM) and Business Process Reengineering (BPR), the two most common approaches to organizational reform in the private sector. The literature suggests that both have failed to generate the desired results two-thirds of the time or more. They concluded, "The hope that we can systematically turn around all troubled schools—or even a majority of them—is at odds with much of what we know from similar efforts in the private sector."

Many have noted that flexibility and dynamism are part of the genetic code of private business, so we should expect these organizations to be more receptive to the massive changes required by a turnaround process than institutions set in what Hess calls the "political, regulatory, and contractual morass of K–12 schooling." Accordingly, school turnarounds should be more difficult to achieve. Indeed, a consultant with the Bridgespan Group reported, "Turnarounds in the public education space are far harder than any turnaround I've ever seen in the for-profit space."

Closing Schools

We shouldn't be surprised then that turnarounds in urban education have largely failed. The surprise and shame is that urban public education, unlike nearly every other industry, profession, and field, has never developed a sensible solution to its continuous failures. After undergoing improvement efforts, a struggling private firm that continues to lose money will close, get taken over, or go bankrupt. Unfit elected officials are voted out of office. The worst lawyers can be disbarred, and the most negligent doctors can lose their licenses. Urban school districts, at long last, need an equivalent.

The beginning of the solution is establishing a clear process for closing schools. The simplest and best way to put this into operation is the charter model. Each school, in conjunction with the state or district, would develop a five-year contract with performance measures. Consistent failure to meet goals in key areas would result in closure. Alternatively, the state could decide that districts only have one option—not five—for schools reaching NCLB-mandated restructuring: closure.

This would have three benefits. First, children would no longer be subjected to schools with long track records of failure and high probabilities of continued failure.

Second, the fear of closure might generate improvement in some low-performing schools. Failure in public education has had fewer consequences (for adults) than in other fields, a fact that might contribute to the persistent struggles of some schools. We should have limited expectations in this regard, however. Even in the private sector, where the consequences for poor performance are significant, some low-performing entities never become successful.

Third, and by far the most important and least appreciated factor, closures make room for replacements, which have a transformative positive impact on the health of a field. When a firm folds due to poor performance, the slack is taken up by the expansion of successful existing firms—meaning that those excelling have the opportunity to do more—or by new firms. New entrants not only fill gaps, they have a tendency to better reflect current market conditions. They are also far likelier to introduce innovations: Google, Facebook, and Twitter were not products of long-standing firms. Certainly not all new starts will excel, not in education, not in any field. But when provided the right characteristics and environment, their potential is vast.

Creative Destruction

The churn caused by closures isn't something to be feared; on the contrary, it's a familiar prerequisite for industry health. Richard Foster and Sarah Kaplan's brilliant 2001 book *Creative Destruction* catalogued the ubiquity of turnover in thriving industries, including the eventual loss of once-dominant players. Churn generates new ideas, ensures responsiveness, facilitates needed change, and empowers the best to do more.

These principles can be translated easily into urban public education via tools already at our fingertips thanks to chartering: start-ups, replications, and expansions. Chartering has enabled new school starts for nearly 20 years and school replications and expansions for a decade. Chartering has demonstrated clearly that the ingredients of healthy, orderly churn can be brought to bear on public education.

A small number of progressive leaders of major urban school systems are using school closure and replacement to transform their long-broken districts: Under Chancellor Joel Klein, New York City has closed nearly 100 traditional public schools and opened more than 300 new schools. In 2004, Chicago announced the Renaissance 2010 project, which is built around closing chronically failing schools and opening 100 new public schools by [2010].

Numerous other big-city districts are in the process of closing troubled schools, including Detroit, Philadelphia, and

Washington, D.C. In Baltimore, under schools CEO Andrés Alonso, reform's guiding principles include "Closing schools that don't work for our kids," "Creating new options that have strong chances of success," and "Expanding some programs that are already proving effective."

Equally encouraging, there are indications that these ideas, which once would have been considered heretical, are being embraced by education's cognoscenti [experts]. A group of leading reformers, the Coalition for Student Achievement, published a document in April 2009 that offered ideas for the best use of the federal government's $100 billion in stimulus funding. They recommended that each state develop a mechanism to "close its lowest performing five percent of schools and replace them with higher-performing, new schools including public charter schools."

A generation ago, few would have believed that such a fundamental overhaul of urban districts was on the horizon, much less that perennial underperformers New York City, Chicago, and Baltimore would be at the front of the pack with much of the education establishment and reform community in tow. But, consciously or not, these cities have begun internalizing the lessons of healthy industries and the chartering mechanism, which, if vigorously applied to urban schooling, have extraordinary potential. Best of all, these districts and outstanding charter leaders like KIPP [Knowledge is Power Program] Houston (with 15 schools already and dozens more planned) and Green Dot (which opened 5 new schools surrounding one of Los Angeles's worst high schools) are showing that the formula boils down to four simple but eminently sensible steps: close failing schools, open new schools, replicate great schools, repeat.

Today's fixation with fix-it efforts is misguided. Turnarounds have consistently shown themselves to be ineffective—truly an unscalable strategy for improving urban districts—and our relentless preoccupation with improving the worst schools actually inhibits the development of a healthy urban public-education industry.

Those hesitant about replacing turnarounds with closures should simply remember that a failed business doesn't indict capitalism and an unseated incumbent doesn't indict democracy. Though temporarily painful, both are essential mechanisms for maintaining long-term systemwide quality, responsiveness, and innovation. Closing America's worst urban schools doesn't indict public education nor does it suggest a lack of commitment to disadvantaged students. On the contrary, it reflects our insistence on finally taking the steps necessary to build city school systems that work for the boys and girls most in need.

> *"School turnarounds are difficult . . . but it's hard to see how simply closing a low-performing school is any solution."*

Failing Schools Should Not Be Closed

Maisie McAdoo

Maisie McAdoo is a writer and researcher for the New York City teachers union. In the following viewpoint, she argues that closing failing schools has not worked in Chicago. Instead, evidence shows that students who leave a closed school generally end up in poorly performing schools and show no improvement in achievement. Closing large high schools can also damage other schools that are then forced to take in a sudden influx of students and can upset students' support systems. McAdoo concludes that failing schools should be fixed with new educational strategies rather than simply closed.

As you read, consider the following questions:

1. According to the study McAdoo cites, following the closing of their schools what percent of Chicago students moved to high-performing schools and what percent enrolled in schools on probation?

2. Based on a report by the Center for New York City Affairs, as cited by the author, what destabilized Jane Addams High School in the Bronx?

3. What are some educational strategies that McAdoo says Allen Odden recommends for failing schools?

School turnarounds are difficult—ask anyone who has been part of one—but it's hard to see how simply closing a low-performing school is any solution.

Still, among those who favor a corporate approach to running school systems, turnarounds are viewed as not worth the investment. Closing low-performing schools has become a solution in and of itself, creating a clean slate that is somehow expected to yield better schools.

"Turnarounds have consistently shown themselves to be ineffective," asserts Andy Smarick, a former [George W.] Bush White House education aide and charter school lobbyist. . . . "[O]ur relentless preoccupation with improving the worst schools actually inhibits the development of a healthy urban public-education industry."

Unsuccessful in Chicago

Smarick doesn't say what should happen with their students, an inconvenience in his scheme. And he evidently hasn't read the research on Chicago's closing schools.

After then-Chicago Schools Superintendent Arne Duncan had shut down 38 "failing" schools in Chicago from 2001 to 2006, he was compelled to shift gears and adopt a "turnaround" approach, according to a new report from the University of Chicago's Consortium on Chicago School Research. Closing schools had had little effect.

In the Chicago report, "When Schools Close," authors Marisa de la Torre and Julia Gwynne examine the impact on the students in these schools. They follow the displaced students, tracking their reading and math achievement, special education referrals, retentions, summer school attendance, mobility and high school performance and comparing them to students in similar schools that did not close.

What did they find?

- Most students who transferred out of closing schools in Chicago wound up in schools that were academically weak—"some of the weakest schools in the system," the authors write. Forty percent enrolled in schools on probation and 42 percent in schools with test scores in the bottom 25 percent. Just 6 percent of displaced students moved to higher-performing schools.

- In the year before the school closed—typically the closing announcements were made in January—students' scores showed a loss of one-and-a-half months of learning in reading and about half a month in math.

- A year after students left the schools, their reading and math achievement was no different. They were also less likely to enroll in summer school and more likely to change schools again.

"Overall, we found few effects, either positive or negative, of school closings on the achievement of displaced students," the authors write.

Here in New York, where the chancellor and mayor have already closed some 100 schools and plan to close many more, researchers have found that shuttering large high schools can do inadvertent damage to other schools.

In "The New Marketplace," a June 2009 report by the Center for New York City Affairs, authors Clara Hemphill and Kim Nauer chronicle the fortunes of Jane Addams HS in the Bronx, a popular and successful vocational school that trained mostly girls for careers in nursing, cosmetology and tourism.

It was badly destabilized by a surge of 200 more students—including many boys who didn't want to be there—from nearby closing schools. Attendance and graduation rates declined dramatically. "They took a really good, functioning building and destroyed it," former Jane Addams Chapter Leader Elliot Gloskin told the authors.

Closing Schools Creates Turmoil

One thing that gets lost in the "close 'em down" furor is that students' lives and support systems can be upended. When Fenger HS in Chicago was closed [in 2009], all the staff—even the custodians—were dismissed, though the students stayed.

"We have relationships with kids who may not even have another adult in their homes or their lives," wrote Deborah Lynch, former Chicago teacher union president who teaches at a school near Fenger. In a letter to the *Chicago Sun Times* Oct. 2 [2009] she said, "How could anyone expect that completely eliminating all the professionals and staff of a tough high-poverty high school could be a good thing?"

And how could anyone expect that motivated, skilled teachers would want to come to work in such a school?

Smarick and his colleagues might lend an ear to Allen Odden, professor of educational leadership at the University of Wisconsin, who has studied schools for some 40 years.

In a commentary in the Dec. 7 [2009] *Education Week* called "We Know How to Turn Schools Around," Odden calls for leaders to implement educational strategies, not just structural ones, to fix struggling schools.

To turn schools around, he says, "Throw out the old curriculum and adopt new textbooks, create new curriculum programs, and start to build, over time, a common understanding of effective instruction ... focus intensely on instructional practices shown to work."

Move beyond "a concentration on state tests," he continues, to use a variety of formative and diagnostic assessments. Create collaborative teacher teams to improve professional development. Make extensive use of expert teachers. "The bot-

Closing Schools Does Not Improve Outcomes

School closings had a negative impact on reading and math achievement the year of the announcement (a few months before the school actually closed). . . . During this announcement year, reading achievement for students in schools slated for closing was about one-and-a-half months of learning below the expected level, and math achievement was more than half a month below the expected level. . . .

Once students left schools slated for closing, there were no additional negative effects on achievement. In fact, one year later, displaced students' reading and math achievement had returned to their expected level. Although displaced students were likely to have experienced some difficulties in adjusting to their new schools, on average these challenges had no apparent impact on their learning. . . .

There were no long-term effects on the math achievement of displaced students. In reading, displaced students were about one-and-a-half months behind in learning two years after their schools closed; however, this difference between their actual learning and their expected learning is not statistically significant. Three years after schools closed, displaced students were about one-and-a-half months ahead of their expected learning in reading; but, again, this difference is not statistically significant.

Marisa de la Torre and Julia Gwynne,
When Schools Close:
Effects on Displaced Students in Chicago Public Schools,
October 2009. http://ccsr.uchicago.edu.

tom line is that the country knows how to turn around low-performing education systems," he concludes.

His recommended strategies aren't easy, and they won't free up real estate for a new charter school. But a closed school is just an empty building. A turnaround school is a community jewel.

| "Educators, children and parents . . . are blamed and shamed as the 'cause' of the educational 'failure' of the very children our society . . . opts instead to segregate, underfund, push out of school, and ignore."

Labeling Schools as Failing Is Unhelpful and Unfair

Lois M. Meyer

Lois M. Meyer is a professor of education at the University of New Mexico. In the following viewpoint she discusses a talk given by writer Jonathan Kozol. Based on his presentation, Meyer argues that emphasizing school failure and standards unfairly stigmatizes poor students and low-income communities. She says that national policies promote segregation and huge income disparities between rich and poor, and she concludes that these unjust policies, not teachers or students, must be confronted. The solution to poor students' problems, she insists, is not more testing, but more activism.

Lois M. Meyer, "Hungering for Educational Justice," susanohanian.org/NCLB Outrages, October 19, 2007. Reproduced by permission.

As you read, consider the following questions:

1. According to Meyer, who were those in the crowd who listened to Jonathan Kozol's talk?

2. What is Jonathan Kozol's book *Letters to a Young Teacher* about, according to the author?

3. What does Kozol say that children care about instead of the global marketplace, as reported by Meyer?

National Book Award-winning author and educator Jonathan Kozol recently explained to an almost overflow audience at the University of New Mexico (UNM) why he appeared thin and weak. For three months he has been on a hunger fast for educational justice. Why? Because he can no longer stomach the gross injustices he witnesses in classrooms and schools across the nation. July 1 [2007], two days after the U.S. Supreme Court reversed *Brown vs. Board of Education*, the historic 1954 decision that outlawed segregated schools and mandated school integration,[1] Kozol began his hunger fast against "the racist agenda inherent in the federal education reform act [No Child Left Behind] signed into law by President [George W.] Bush in 2002." His hunger strike is partial—he supplements a liquid diet with some solid nourishment at his doctor's request to sustain life. But, he added, "I'm old now so I'm not afraid to do or say what I believe is right."

Justice, Not Test Scores

We don't hear much about hunger strikes these days. Obesity, sure, bulimia, maybe, but not hunger strikes. Our appetite for the likes of [television shows] *American Idol* and *Desperate Housewives* seems insatiable, while the idea of self-inflicted hunger as a principled act of political protest and personal conviction causes us intellectual if not gastric distress. Fasting

1. In June 2007 the Supreme Court ended voluntary desegregation programs that had been initiated to comply with *Brown*.

for justice seems way more extreme than [the television show] *Extreme Makeover*. Non-violent hunger fasts may have helped [Indian independence leader Mohandas] Gandhi and [Mexican American labor leader] Cesar Chavez tumble colonial empires and unionize California lettuce fields, but that was decades ago. Today both nonviolence and hunger fasting seem to have been deleted from our consciousness and from our menu of possible political actions.

And fasting for educational justice? How would that improve the test scores of low achieving children, or help failing schools meet Adequate Yearly Progress (AYP)? In this age of No Child Left Behind (NCLB), even our concept of educational justice is so shrunken and deformed by government spin that we act as though test scores—rather than children's creativity and excitement about learning, or the priorities and cultural rights of parents and communities—are what matter.

Many in the UNM crowd of new and experienced teachers, school administrators, university students and professors, and concerned parents, were familiar with what Kozol has said and done in the past. He has worked in inner-city schools for more than 40 years, giving voice to children's experiences of public schooling in disturbing books such as *Death at an Early Age, The Shame of the Nation,* and *Savage Inequalities.* His newest book, *Letters to a Young Teacher,* recounts his year-long dialogue with an inexperienced first-grade teacher in a segregated Black school in his home town, Boston. In it he promises to describe "the joys and challenges and passionate rewards of a beautiful profession"—teaching.

Inequality Is to Blame

Kozol made good on his promise, and in doing so, he fed a deep hunger in the audience that night. Public school teachers are hungry to hear a public figure of Kozol's stature commend them with awe and pride and gratitude for their skills and commitment to teaching. NCLB lays the blame for children's

Teachers Are Not the Problem

The justification for [No Child Left Behind] was the presumptuous and ignorant determination by the White House that our urban schools are, for the most part, staffed by mediocre drones who will suddenly become terrific teachers if we place a sword of terror just above their heads and threaten them with penalties if they do not pump their students' scores. . . . There are some mediocre teachers in our schools . . . but hopelessly dull and unimaginative teachers do not suddenly turn into classroom wizards under a regimen that transforms their classrooms into test-prep factories.

Jonathan Kozol,
"Why I Am Fasting: An Explanation to My Friends,"
Huffington Post, *September 10, 2007. www.huffingtonpost.com.*

poor test scores on teachers and schools, and by implication, on parents and communities, especially poor communities of color. It ignores mounds of data that document the increasing inequalities among communities and social classes in family income, health supports, even basics like adequate food and housing, all factors that influence performance on achievement tests and students' opportunities to learn. Instead, NCLB's single-minded and simplistic solution to educational inequalities is to hold educators, children and parents "accountable." In other words, they are blamed and shamed as the "cause" of the educational "failure" of the very children our society refuses to insure and opts instead to segregate, underfund, push out of school, and ignore.

In stark contrast, Kozol celebrated the contributions of education professionals as the strength and soul of public education. He encouraged especially young teachers and those who are preparing to teach: "Teachers I meet today are some of the most gifted and enthusiastic I have ever seen. Especially those who teach young children should not permit themselves to be drill sergeants of the State or trainers for corporate global capitalism."

Children command most of Kozol's attention, real children with names like Pineapple and Ariel and Shaniqua who populate the classrooms where he visits and volunteers time. He denounced the educational injustices these children endure in the wealthiest and most powerful nation on earth—resegregated schools; overcrowded classrooms; narrow, test-driven curricula; rote, drill-and-kill teaching methods. Though labeled by NCLB as "failures," the spirit of these children is inspiring—most still hunger to learn.

The federal law's misplaced, child-damaging priorities are masked in deceptive rhetoric about "standards" and "excellence" and "global competitiveness." NCLB pretends to address quality education for children but its real concerns are different. "Why should kindergartners care about the global marketplace?" Kozol demands. "They care about bellybuttons and elbows and furry caterpillars." Curiosity about their world and joy in discovery, not test scores or world markets, are what propel young children to learn.

Some words never appear in NCLB at all, "words like curiosity, creativity, laughter, and delight." Some parents and communities, and undoubtedly legislators, can demand for their children the best education money can buy, an education that still challenges and delights. But too many Black and Hispanic and Native American kids, and those with special needs or those who are still learning English, are force-fed a stripped down, debased and test-driven curriculum. Kozol's conclusion was unflinching: "It is deeply hypocritical to hold 8 or 9 year olds accountable for their academic achievement but not hold Congressional delegates and the president accountable for not providing poor kids with the same education they themselves insist on giving to their own kids."

Focus on Children

Syndicated columnist Ruben Navarrette Jr.'s recent column ("Dismantle No Child Left Behind and Watch Us Fail", Oct. 1 [2007]) is a stark example of the deceptive education talk fueled by NCLB. Navarrette claimed to speak in defense of the needs and wants of children "who don't vote, or give money, or twist arms, or pay union dues." Yet Navarrette never talked about children at all, not about their feelings, their interests, their dreams, or their reaction to being labeled as "failures." Instead, Navarrette's column berates teachers unions, the Democratic-controlled Congress, and "certain Republicans" for seeking to eliminate the most punitive NCLB requirements. Navarrette applauded U.S. Education Secretary Margaret Spellings as a "ferocious defender" of NCLB.

Ferociously defending NCLB is a far cry from defending children and quality instruction and educational justice for all. Kozol understands, as did Gandhi and Chavez before him, that hunger for educational justice demands principled political action if we are to dismantle federal education legislation that intellectually starves our neediest children.

Periodical Bibliography

The following articles have been selected to supplement the diverse views presented in this chapter.

Stephanie Banchero	"Daley School Plan Fails to Make Grade," *Chicago Tribune*, January 17, 2010.
Seyward Darby	"The New Republic: Is Education Reform All Talk?" NPR Online, Febraury 8, 2010. www.npr.org.
Sam Dillon	"Report Questions Duncan's Policy of Closing Failing Schools," *New York Times*, October 28, 2009.
Arne Duncan	"Turning Around the Bottom Five Percent," U.S. Department of Education, June 22, 2009. www2.ed.gov.
FairTest	"Paying Teachers for Student Test Scores Damages Schools and Undermines Learning," November 19, 2009. www.fairtest.org.
Pamela Felcher	"Don't Judge Teachers by Test Scores," *Los Angeles Times*, March 26, 2008.
Zach Miners	"Obama Looks at Closing (and Reopening) Failing Schools," *On Education*, May 14, 2009.
Amanda Ripley	"What Makes a Great Teacher," *Atlantic*, January–February 2010.
Thomas Toch	"Measure for Measure," *Washington Monthly*, October–November 2005.
Marcus A. Winters	"Grading Teachers," *National Review*, September 16, 2009.

OPPOSING
VIEWPOINTS®
SERIES

CHAPTER 4

What Role Should School Choice Play in School Reform?

Chapter Preface

Charter schools are schools that receive public money but are freed from certain state standards in return for being subject to specified kinds of accountability. Charter schools are seen as promoting school choice since students usually apply, or enter a lottery, to attend charter schools.

The largest and perhaps most successful chain of charter schools in the United States is a group of middle schools known as the Knowledge Is Power Program, or KIPP. KIPP was founded in inner-city Houston in 1994 and was specifically aimed at preparing underachieving and minority students for a college education. The two original academies, according to the history page on the KIPP Web site were KIPP Academy Middle School in Houston and KIPP Academy in the South Bronx, New York.

KIPP's program includes extended school days, school weeks, and school years. Students go to school "between nine and nine-and-a-half hours" a day, as opposed to the typical seven-hour day at normal public schools, according to Larry Abramson, writing on the National Public Radio Web site on September 8, 2009. The KIPP Web site also notes that the schools "relentlessly focus on high student performance on standardized tests and other objective measures."

Many commentators have praised KIPP's combination of hard work and accountability. Rehema Ellis, writing on the MSNBC blog The Daily Nightly, visited a KIPP school in the Harlem neighborhood of New York City and said that she found "devotion from everyone: teachers, students, parents, the principal, secretaries, cafeteria and maintenance staff." Charles Upton Sahm, writing in *City Journal* on March 13, 2009, noted that on state math tests in New York, 94 percent of KIPP students scored at or above grade level, in comparison to only 60 percent scoring at or above grade level in the state as a whole. Sahm added that in New York, Washington, Baltimore, San Jose (California), and New Orleans, "the top-performing public middle school is a KIPP school."

Despite such successes, some commentators maintain doubts about KIPP schools. In a March 18, 2009, essay in the *Washington Post*, Jay Matthews, a proponent of KIPP schools, notes that the schools are centered around strong leaders and that "when KIPP school leaders are not doing well, the schools will have trouble." Critics have also argued that KIPP may keep its test scores high by driving away lower-performing students. In a June 8, 2007, article in *Education Week*, Erik W. Robelen noted that in KIPP schools in San Francisco, "fewer than half the fifth graders who entered three new middle schools in 2003" were still enrolled in 2007. The fact that poor students drop out may tend to inflate the overall test scores of some KIPP schools.

Despite such concerns, however, KIPP is seen overall as one of the signal achievements of the charter school movement. The following viewpoints will look at the pros and cons of other efforts to promote school choice in the United States.

"Opportunity Scholarships [vouchers] can give [students] a real chance to receive a quality education."

Vouchers Help Students Get a Better Education

Dan Lips

Dan Lips is education analyst at the Heritage Foundation. In the following viewpoint, he argues in favor of scholarships and tuition vouchers to allow students in failing public schools the opportunity to attend private schools. Lips argues that such programs have succeeded in the past, that they are popular with families who participate in them, and that they help low-income students receive a better education.

As you read, consider the following questions:

1. What must schools that fail to meet goals of yearly progress for two years offer low-income students, according to Lips?

2. Why does the author believe that giving more money to poor schools is not a good solution for students?

3. According to Lips, how did eighth graders at Thurgood Marshall Middle School in Baltimore do on state tests?

L ast week [in April 2006], Education Secretary Margaret Spellings unveiled a new school choice proposal aimed at helping low-income children trapped in underperforming public schools. In New York alone, where Secretary Spellings delivered her speech, an estimated 125,000 students attend persistently failing public schools. President [George W.] Bush's proposal would give thousands of these children—and their peers throughout the nation—the ability to attend a better school.

Failing Schools

"More than 1,700 schools around the country have failed to meet state standards for five or six years in a row," Spellings explained. "We're proposing a new $100 million Opportunity Scholarships Fund to help low-income students in these schools attend the private school of their choice or receive intensive one-on-one tutoring." Thousands of students throughout the nation stand to benefit from such a program if the legislation is passed by Congress.

According to preliminary estimates, 170,000 students in Los Angeles are attending persistently failing public schools as defined by the [federal educational reform] No Child Left Behind (NCLB) act of 2002. In other large districts, such as Chicago (120,000), Philadelphia (63,000), Baltimore (23,000), and Memphis (16,000), thousands of students are enrolled in persistently failing schools and would be eligible to participate in the administration's Opportunity Scholarship program.

The Secretary's speech followed the release of a new Department of Education report on the implementation of No Child Left Behind, which showed that participation in the existing school choice programs remains low. Under No Child Left Behind, schools that fail to meet goals of adequate yearly progress for two years must offer low-income students the option to transfer to a better public school. Schools that fail for three years must offer low-income students after-school tutoring. Less than one percent of 3.9 million eligible students took advantage of the opportunity to transfer to an alternative public school. A higher, though fairly small, percentage (17 percent of 1.4 million eligible students) utilized the after-school tutoring provisions of NCLB.

One of the main reasons for the low participation rates in the NCLB school choice provisions is the failure of school systems to implement the program and communicate its benefits. The Department of Education found that half of all school districts notified parents about the public school choice option after the school year had already started, when few parents would want to change their child's school. Secretary Spellings is ordering a review of states' compliance with the school choice provisions and warns that "withholding federal funds" is a possible consequence for states that fail to meet this responsibility.

More Choice Needed

Yet, even if the transfer and tutoring provisions of the earlier legislation were implemented perfectly, they would still only help children at the margins and would limit their enrollment options to choices within the public school system. Unfortunately, in some communities there are few open seats in high quality public schools. The opportunity scholarships initiative would provide children with expanded options of authentic school choice.

The plan is similar to the new federal school voucher[1] program for Washington D.C., through which 1,700 low-income children have been able to attend private school. The D.C. voucher program has steadily gained popularity among

---

1. School tuition vouchers are certificates issued by the government, which parents can use to pay for a private school for their children.

families. According to the Washington Scholarship Fund, there were approximately two applicants for every available scholarship. In all, the Bush administration's Opportunity Scholarships initiative could fund private-school scholarships for more than 20,000 low-income children in cities across the nation.

Opponents of school choice will likely argue—as they have against other school choice programs—that, rather than providing vouchers, funds should be used to fix the failing public school system. But children trapped in failing schools cannot afford to wait until they are somehow brought up to par. Even under the President's proposed Opportunity Scholarship program, eligible students are attending schools that have already failed to meet state standards for six or more years. If anything, this proposal doesn't go far enough in rescuing students from substandard schools.

Consider the track record of Thurgood Marshall Middle School in Baltimore, Maryland—a school that would qualify for the administration's program—where 75 percent of the 795 students are from economically disadvantaged families. There, according to a report by Standard and Poors [a company that analyzes and evaluates school data], less than 2 percent of all 8th graders achieved "proficient" scores on the state's math test and just 21 percent had "proficient" scores in reading. How much longer must children in this school wait?

Like the children of Thurgood Marshall Middle School, students in the 1,700 persistently failing public schools throughout the nation deserve help right now. Opportunity Scholarships can give them a real chance to receive a quality education—a chance that only real school choice can provide.

> *"What will improve our schools [are] smaller classes and better curricula. Vouchers take us away from those essential goals."*

Vouchers Do Little to Improve Individual Student Achievement

Jason Barnosky

Jason Barnosky is coeditor of the book Counting Kids: Children and the Study of Public Policy and Politics. *In the following viewpoint, he argues that voucher programs have done little to improve student learning. Barnosky points to the extensive experience with vouchers in Chile, where twenty years of voucher use seem to have done little to increase test scores despite a widespread move from public to private schools. Barnosky concludes that the solution to better schools is smaller classes and better curricula, not vouchers.*

As you read, consider the following questions:

1. According to Barnosky, what group has most consistently showed small academic gains from voucher programs?

2. What expected changes in school enrollment does Barnosky say occurred in Chile following the introduction of the voucher program?

3. According to Hseih and Urquiola, as cited by the author, how did the voucher program in Chile affect the number of students who repeated a grade?

With President [George W.] Bush's encouragement, Congress passed a provision in last week's [February 6, 2004,] budget for a $14 million voucher program in Washington, D.C.—the first such federally financed program in the country. While the president and Congress may think that jumping on the voucher bandwagon is the best way to improve our nation's schools, little indicates that they're right. Our experiences with voucher programs have so far been disappointing, and a look at Chile—a country that has had a nationwide voucher program in place for more than 20 years—suggests that they won't get better with time.

Milton Friedman and Vouchers

Decades ago, [Nobel Prize–winning economist] Milton Friedman popularized the idea of school vouchers. His idea was straightforward: Provide parents with a voucher for a specified amount of money and allow them to redeem it at the public or private school of their choice. Schools would be put to the tests of the market, and the educational system would improve. The idea lay more or less dormant in the United States until the 1990s, when several cities set up small programs. Studies and experiments followed, but the results haven't matched the high hopes.

Supporters can point to a few things. Parents of children in voucher programs, for instance, are much happier with their children's schools. But on the most crucial factor, academic achievement, there hasn't been much to brag about. The most consistent findings have been modest academic achievement among African Americans and a lack of evidence one way or the other for everyone else. These consistent findings, however, have included a consistent caveat: More time and research is needed. When we turn to Chile, we see that there's not much to look forward to.

Chile adopted its voucher program in the years following Augusto Pinochet's 1973 coup, coming closer than any other country to realizing Friedman's vision. Pre-reform, the Chilean school system was heavily centralized. The Ministry of Education was responsible for financing and management. It devised the curriculum for the entire schools system, decided who was hired, and determined how much they would make. The system that replaced it in the early 1980s did away with nearly all of this.

Administration of the public schools was transferred out of the Ministry of Education and into the hands of local municipalities, eliminating top-down management. Students were given vouchers if they wished to attend private schools, and public-school funding became dependent on student enrollment. Vouchers could be used at religious schools, and families with the means could opt out of the system entirely and attend tuition-only schools (voucher-accepting private schools couldn't charge tuition).

Some things have gone as expected. Students moved out of the public schools and into private ones. Public-school enrollment fell from 80 percent in the 1970s to below 60 percent in the 1990s. And private schools responded to the increase in demand. Their numbers increased by roughly 30 percent from 1982 to 1995.

No Academic Improvement

But in a recent paper evaluating the Chilean voucher program, Chang-Tai Hseih and Miguel Urquiola of the National Bureau of Economic Research find no evidence that the reforms have improved academic achievement. Looking at 150 communities throughout the country, Hseih and Urquiola found that increases in private-school enrollment had no affect on average math and language test scores. Repetition rates—defined in Chile as the number of students who have repeated the same grade twice—actually grew worse as more students attended private schools. Hseih and Urquiola also looked at the country's performance in international tests and found that Chilean students seem to be performing slightly worse than they were 30 years ago.

Meanwhile, Patrick McEwan has found that while the Catholic schools seem to perform slightly better than the public schools, the voucher-friendly private schools do, at best, as well as the public schools, and sometimes less so. A few studies have argued that the private voucher schools actually perform better than the public ones. But it's worth pointing out that these schools don't have to accept every student who applies—a luxury the public schools don't have. Private schools can, and do, skim the better ones. What's surprising is that even with this advantage, they haven't pulled clearly ahead.

The failure of the Chilean program to make great strides could be attributed to the design of the policies. Perhaps the incentives aren't structured the right way. Despite the decrease in demand for public schools, for example, few have closed over the years. But even if the voucher program is flawed, overall student achievement for the country should have improved as more students moved into the private sector. And, as Hseih and Urquiola show, this just hasn't happened. Examining the consequences of the Chilean reforms, it's hard to argue that vouchers have done much to improve the educational system of the country. And they suggest that 20 years down the line, the results of America's voucher experiments will look much as they do today: disappointing.

The trouble with these policies goes beyond their mediocrity. We already have a pretty good idea of what will improve our schools: smaller classes and better curricula. Vouchers take us away from these essential goals and carry us toward a new set of problems, such as the possibility of increased racial and economic segregation. While school-choice proponents undoubtedly see Congress' decision as a landmark, it's actually a setback.

| *"Evidence consistently supports the con-clusion that vouchers improve public schools."*

School Vouchers Help to Reform Public Schools

Greg Forster

Greg Forster is a senior fellow at the Friedman Foundation for Educational Choice and coauthor, with Joy P. Greene, of the book Education Myths: What Special-Interest Groups Want You to Believe About Our Schools—and Why It Isn't So. *In the following viewpoint, he argues that empirical research studies consistently show that public schools improve when voucher programs are introduced. He suggests that this is mainly the result of increased competition. He concludes that Americans need to become more accustomed to the idea of competition in schools, just as they are accustomed to competition when they shop for most other goods and services.*

As you read, consider the following questions:

1. How does Forster explain the single study in Washington, D.C., that found that vouchers had no positive impact on public schools?

Greg Forster, "Introduction," *School Choice Issues In Depth: A Win-Win Solution: The Empirical Evidence on How Vouchers Affect Public Schools,* The Friedman Foundation for Educational Choice, February 2009. Reproduced by permission.

2. According to the author, how much money did school choice programs save between 1990 and 2006?

3. What examples does Forster provide of situations in which Americans rely on competition among nonprofit service providers?

Contrary to the widespread claim that vouchers[1] hurt public schools, ... empirical evidence consistently supports the conclusion that vouchers improve public schools. No empirical study has ever found that vouchers had a negative impact on public schools.

There are a variety of explanations for why vouchers might improve public schools, the most important being that competition from vouchers introduces healthy incentives for public schools to improve. . . .

Evidence of Voucher Success

- A total of 17 empirical studies have examined how vouchers affect academic achievement in public schools. Of these studies, 16 find that vouchers improved public schools and one finds no visible impact. No empirical studies find that vouchers harm public schools.

- Vouchers can have a significant positive impact on public schools without necessarily producing visible changes in the overall performance of a large city's schools. The overall performance of a large school system is subject to countless different influences, and only careful study using sound scientific methods can isolate the impact of vouchers from all other factors so it can be accurately measured. Thus, the absence of dramatic "miracle" results in cities with voucher programs has no bearing on the question of whether

1. School tuition vouchers are certificates issued by the government, which parents can use to pay for a private school for their children.

vouchers have improved public schools; only scientific analysis can answer that question.

- Every empirical study ever conducted in Milwaukee, Florida, Ohio, Texas, Maine and Vermont finds that voucher programs in those places improved public schools.

- The single study conducted in Washington, D.C. is the only study that found no visible impact from vouchers. This is not surprising, since the D.C. voucher program is the only one designed to shield public schools from the impact of competition. Thus, the D.C. study does not detract from the research consensus in favor of a positive effect from voucher competition.

- Alternative explanations such as "stigma effect" [which suggests that failing schools improve to avoid a stigma rather than because of vouchers] and "regression to the mean" [which suggests that failing schools improve because they simply cannot get much worse] do not account for the positive effects identified in these studies. When these alternative explanations have been evaluated empirically, the evidence has not supported them. . . .

Choice Is Good

School vouchers, which allow parents to use public funds to send their children to the school of their choice, public or private, are among the most prominent and successful reforms in the education field. Perhaps the single most important question about vouchers is how they impact public schools. There are many people who agree that vouchers are good for the students who have the opportunity to use them, but are concerned about how vouchers impact the quality of education for other students who remain in public schools.

Vouchers Improve Public School Performance

Empirical studies finding that vouchers...

	...improved public school outcomes	...didn't visibly change public school outcomes	...hurt public school outcomes
Milwaukee	5	0	0
Florida	10	0	0
Other programs	3	0	0
Washington D.C.	0	1	0

A total of 17 studies are represented here; figures do not sum to 17 because some studies include findings on more than one program.

TAKEN FROM: Greg Forster, *A Win-Win Solution: The Empirical Evidence on How Vouchers Affect Public Schools*, Friedman Foundation, February 2009.

Defenders of the government monopoly on schools frequently claim that vouchers harm public schools. They claim that vouchers drain money and "cream" the best students. Voucher proponents, on the other hand, argue that vouchers improve public schools. They point to evidence that vouchers save money for public school budgets rather than "draining" money, and that vouchers do not only send the best students to private schools. The proponents argue that vouchers allow students to find the right schools to serve their individual needs, and introduce competition for students that creates healthy incentives that are lacking in the existing government school monopoly.

A large body of empirical evidence speaks to this question. There are now 24 school choice programs in 14 states and Washington, D.C. Over 160,000 students use these programs to attend private schools using public funds. The effects of these programs have been studied using scientific methods and are no longer the subject of mere speculation and anecdotal observation. . . .

Unfortunately, Americans are not accustomed to thinking of K–12 education in terms of choice. They expect and demand the right to select their own goods and services in everything from food, housing, clothing, transportation and medical care to magazines, haircuts, dry cleaning and video games. If government attempted to assign people to live in certain neighborhoods or shop at certain grocery stores, they would howl in protest. Americans even expect and demand choice when it comes to education outside of K–12 schools—everywhere from colleges to trade schools to night classes. But when it comes to K–12 education, the idea that they would choose for themselves rather than having government dictate what they receive is new and sometimes uncomfortable.

This helps to explain why many Americans readily accept claims about school vouchers that are empirically false or poorly reasoned. For example, when teachers unions claim that vouchers "drain money" from public schools, many Americans nod in agreement. But how would those same people respond if they were told that from now on they would have to receive all their medical care from a doctor assigned to them by the government, rather than from their current family doctor, on grounds that their choice to seek care from their current doctor "drains money" from the budget of the doctor chosen by the government?

Competition Improves Schools

In fact, vouchers make public schools better off financially, rather than worse off. When students leave public schools using vouchers, not all the funding associated with those students goes with them. This means public schools are left with more money to serve the students who remain. State budgets also benefit because educating students in private schools rather than public schools not only accomplishes better results, it also costs less. From 1990 to 2006, the nation's school choice programs saved a total of $422 million for local school districts and $22 million for state budgets.

Similarly, the claim that vouchers "cream" the best students from public schools has no empirical evidence to support it. The best available analyses of this question have found voucher applicants to be very similar to the population of students eligible for vouchers in terms of demographics and educational background. In the Washington, D.C. voucher program, applicants were very similar to a representative sample of the eligible population citywide not only in terms of demographics, but also in their baseline test scores.

Meanwhile, for similar reasons, the idea that vouchers might improve public schools seems counter-intuitive to many Americans. In fact, it is not hard to explain why vouchers would be expected to improve public schools. One reason is because vouchers allow parents to find the right particular school for each individual child. Every child is unique and has unique educational needs.

The Importance of Accountability

But probably the most important reason vouchers would improve public schools is because they give parents a meaningful way to hold schools accountable for their performance. Under the current system, if a school isn't doing a good job, the only ways to get a better school—purchase private schooling or move to a new neighborhood—are prohibitively expensive or cumbersome for many families. These options are especially difficult for low-income and disadvantaged students.

Thus, in the absence of parental choice, schools lack the positive incentive for better performance that most other types of service institutions take for granted. Hospitals know they must do a good job or else lose patients. Colleges must provide a good education (and other services and opportunities that parents expect from colleges) or else lose students. Professionals like doctors and lawyers must provide good services or else lose clients. Stores must provide good value or else lose customers.

With vouchers, those positive incentives we take for granted everywhere else are provided for schools. If a public school is providing adequate services, parents can leave their children where they are and be no worse off. But if not, parents can choose a private school that will serve their children better. Either way, schools know that parents have the power to hold them accountable.

The same Americans who have difficulty with the idea that competition improves schools have no difficulty applying the same concept everywhere else. They know that monopolies provide poor quality because they have little incentive to serve their clients well. And when they get bad service, they say, "I'll take my business elsewhere" because they know that this provides an incentive for better service.

They do this even in fields like medical care where the service providers have other motives besides profit-seeking for being in the fields they're in. If a hospital is losing patients because it provides poor care, that loss of patients will provide a motive to improve care regardless of whether the hospital is for-profit or non-profit—and the patients know it. So it isn't as though people are only accustomed to thinking this way about profit-seeking businesses.

This lack of connection between what Americans think about choice and competition in K–12 education and what [they] think about choice and competition in virtually every other aspect of life is a great hindrance to accurate public discussion of school vouchers. One good hope for rectifying that problem is to make the public aware of the large body of empirical research that examines how vouchers impact public schools.

| "The evidence is pretty meager that competition from vouchers is making public schools better."

School Vouchers Alone Cannot Reform Public Schools

Sol Stern

Sol Stern is a contributing editor of City Journal *and the author of* Breaking Free: Public School Lessons and the Imperative of School Choice. *In the following viewpoint, he argues that, although school vouchers have helped individual students, they have not caused widespread reform in public schools. Stern concludes that reformers need to focus not just on choice and market incentives, but also on changing classroom practices to better reflect the latest educational research.*

As you read, consider the following questions:

1. According to Stern, how many students receive tax-funded school vouchers?

2. How does the author explain the fact that teacher education is governed by markets but is, in his view, ineffective?

3. To what does Massachusetts owe its educational improvements, according to Stern?

I began writing about school choice in [the New York urban policy magazine] *City Journal* [in the late 1990s]. I believed then (as I still believe) that giving tuition vouchers[1] to poor inner-city students stuck in lousy public schools was a civil rights imperative. Starting in the 1980s, major empirical studies by sociologist James Coleman and other scholars showed that urban Catholic schools were better than public schools at educating the poor, despite spending far less per student. Among the reasons for this superiority: most Catholic educators still believed in a coherent, content-based curriculum, and they enforced order in the classroom. It seemed immoral to keep disadvantaged kids locked up in dismal, future-darkening public schools when vouchers could send them to high-performing Catholic ones—especially when middle-class parents enjoyed education options galore for their children.

Choice Is Not a Panacea

But like other reformers, I also believed that vouchers would force the public schools to improve or lose their student "customers." Since competition worked in other areas, wouldn't it lead to progress in education, too? Maybe Catholic schools' success with voucher students would even encourage public schools to exchange the failed "progressive education" approaches used in most classrooms for the pedagogy that made the Catholic institutions so effective.

"Choice *is* a panacea," argued education scholars John Chubb and Terry Moe in their influential 1990 book *Politics, Markets and America's Schools*. For a time, I thought so, too. Looking back from today's vantage point, it is clear that the school choice movement has been very good for the disadvan-

---

1. School tuition vouchers are certificates issued by the government, which parents can use to pay for a private school for their children.

taged. Public and privately funded voucher programs have liberated hundreds of thousands of poor minority children from failing public schools. The movement has also reshaped the education debate. Not only vouchers, but also charter schools,[2] tuition tax credits, mayoral control, and other reforms are now on the table as alternatives to bureaucratic, special-interest-choked, big-city school systems.

Yet social-change movements need to be attentive to the facts on the ground. Recent developments in both public and Catholic schools suggest that markets in education may not be a panacea—and that we should reexamine the direction of school reform.

Voucher Programs Have Stalled

One such development: taxpayer-funded voucher programs for poor children, long considered by many of us to be the most promising of education reforms, have hit a wall. In 2002, after a decade of organizing by school choice activists, only two programs existed: one in Milwaukee, the other in Cleveland, allowing 17,000 poor students to attend private (mostly Catholic) schools. That year, in *Zelman v. Simmons-Harris*, the Supreme Court ruled that limited voucher programs involving religious schools were compatible with the First Amendment's establishment clause.[3] The 5–4 decision seemed like school choice's Magna Charta [a thirteenth-century legal document that established new freedoms in England]. But the legal victory has led to few real gains. Today, fewer than 25,000 students—compared with a nationwide public school enrollment of 50 million—receive tax-funded vouchers, with a tiny Washington, D.C., program joining those of the other two cities.

Proposals for voucher programs have suffered five straight crushing defeats in state referenda—most recently in Utah, by

2. Charter schools receive public money, but have different programs and accountability than most public schools. Students generally apply for or choose to attend them.
3. The First Amendment of the U.S. Constitution prohibits congress from establishing a state religion. This is sometimes referred to as separation of church and state.

a margin of 62 percent to 38 percent. After each loss, school choice groups blamed the lobbying money poured into the states by teachers' unions, the deceptive ads run by voucher foes, and sometimes even voters' commitment to their children. When the Utah results came in, the principal funder of the pro-voucher side, businessman Patrick Byrne, opined that the voters failed "a statewide IQ test" and that they "don't care enough about their kids." If vouchers can't pass voter scrutiny in conservative Utah, though, how probable is it that they will do so anywhere else? And denouncing voters doesn't seem like a smart way to revive the voucher cause.

Voucher prospects have also dimmed because of the Catholic schools' deepening financial crisis. Without an abundant supply of good, low-cost urban Catholic schools to receive voucher students, voucher programs will have a hard time getting off the ground, let alone succeeding. But cash-strapped Catholic Church officials are closing the Church's inner-city schools at an accelerating rate. With just one Catholic high school left in all of Detroit, for instance, where would the city's disadvantaged students use vouchers even if they had them?

Even more discouraging, vouchers may not be enough to save the Catholic schools that are voucher students' main destination. Archbishop Donald Wuerl of Washington, D.C., recently announced plans to close seven of the district's 28 remaining Catholic schools, all of which are receiving aid from federally funded tuition vouchers, unless the D.C. public school system agreed to take them over and convert them into charter schools. In Milwaukee, several Catholic schools have also closed, or face the threat of closing, despite boosting enrollments with voucher kids.

During the 15 years since the first voucher program got under way in Milwaukee, university researchers have extensively scrutinized the dynamics of school choice and the effect of competition on public schools. The preponderance of studies have shown clear benefits, both academically and otherwise, for the voucher kids. It's gratifying that the research confirms the moral and civil rights argument for vouchers.

But sadly—and this is a second development that reformers must face up to—the evidence is pretty meager that competition from vouchers is making public schools better. When I reported on the Milwaukee voucher experiment in 1999, some early indicators suggested that competition was having just that effect. Members of Milwaukee's school board, for example, said that voucher schools had prompted new reforms in the public school system, including modifying the seniority provisions of the teachers' contract and allowing principals more discretion in hiring. A few public schools began offering phonics-based reading instruction [in which the sounds of letters and words are emphasized in reading instruction] in the early grades, the method used in neighboring Catholic schools. Milwaukee public schools' test scores also improved—and did so most dramatically in those schools under the greatest threat of losing students to vouchers, according to a study by Harvard economist Caroline Hoxby.

Unfortunately, the gains fizzled. Fifteen years into the most expansive school choice program tried in any urban school district in the country, Milwaukee's public schools still suffer from low achievement and miserable graduation rates, with test scores flattening in recent years. Violence and disorder throughout the system seem as serious as ever. Most voucher students are still benefiting, true; but no "Milwaukee miracle," no transformation of the public schools, has taken place. One of the Milwaukee voucher program's founders, African-American educator Howard Fuller, recently told the *Milwaukee Journal Sentinel*, "I think that any honest assessment would have to say that there hasn't been the deep, wholesale improvement in MPS [Milwaukee public schools] that we would have thought." And the lead author of one of the Milwaukee voucher studies, Harvard political scientist Paul Peterson, told me: "The research on school choice programs clearly shows that low-income students benefit academically. It's less clear that the presence of choice in a community motivates public schools to improve."

School Reformers Must Reassess

What should we do about these new realities? Obviously, private scholarship programs ought to keep helping poor families find alternatives to failing public schools. And we can still hope that some legislature, somewhere in America, will vote for another voucher plan, or generous tuition tax credits, before more Catholic schools close. But does the school choice movement have a realistic Plan B for the millions of urban students who will remain stuck in terrible public schools?

According to Hoxby and Peterson, perhaps the two most respected school choice scholars in the country, no such plan is necessary. In their view, the best hope for education improvement continues to be a maximum degree of parental choice—vouchers if possible, but also charter schools and tuition tax credits—plus merit-pay schemes for teachers and accountability systems that distinguish productive from unproductive school principals.

That "incentivist" outlook remains dominant within school reform circles. But a challenge from what one could call "instructionists"—those who believe that curriculum change and good teaching are essential to improving schools—is growing, as a unique public debate sponsored by the Koret Task Force on K–12 Education revealed. Founded in 1999, the Koret Task Force represents a national all-star team of education reform scholars. Permanent fellows include not only Hoxby and Peterson but also Chubb, Moe, education historian Diane Ravitch, Thomas B. Fordham Foundation president Chester Finn, Stanford University economics [professor] Eric Hanushek, and the guru of "cultural literacy," [the idea that reading comprehension requires wide background knowledge.] E.D. Hirsch, Jr. (recently retired). Almost from the start, the Koret scholars divided into incentivist and instructionist camps. "We have had eight years and we haven't been able to agree," says Hoxby. But in early 2007, members did agree to hold a debate at the group's home, the Hoover Institution at Stanford University: "Resolved: True School Reform Demands More Attention to Curriculum and Instruction than to Markets and Choice." Hirsch and Ravitch argued the affirmative, Hoxby and Peterson the negative.

Hirsch and Ravitch opened by saying that while they had no opposition to charter schools or other forms of choice, charter schools had produced "disappointing results." Try a thought experiment, urged Ravitch. Say that one school system features market incentives and unlimited choices for parents and students, but no standard curriculum. Then posit another system, with no choice allowed, but in which the educational leadership enforces a rich curriculum and favors effective instructional approaches. In the market system, Ravitch predicted, "most schools will reflect the dominant ideas of the schools of education, where most teachers get their training, so most schools will adopt programs of whole language and fuzzy math. . . . Most students under a pure choice regime will know very little about history or literature or science." The system with the first-rate curriculum and effective pedagogy, Ravitch argued, would produce better education outcomes.

Responding, Peterson and Hoxby paid respects to good curricula and instructional methods. But the key question, in their view, was who would *decide* which curricula and instructional methods were best. Here, the pro-choice debaters made no bones about it: the market's "invisible hand" was the way to go. As Hoxby put it, educational choice would erect a "bulwark against special-interest groups hijacking the curriculum."

Competition Has Limits

I had supported the competition argument for school choice as a working hypothesis, but my doubts about it grew after recent results from the Milwaukee experiment, and nothing said in the Koret debate restored my confidence. And something else caught my attention: Ravitch's comment about "the dominant ideas of the schools of education, where most teachers get their training." The statement slipped by, unchallenged by the incentivist side.

While the arguments about school choice and markets swirled during the past 15 years, both Ravitch and Hirsch wrote landmark books (*Left Back* and *The Schools We Need and Why We Don't Have Them*, respectively) on how the nation's education schools have built an "impregnable fortress" (Hirsch's words) of wrong ideas and ineffective classroom practices that teachers then carry into America's schools, almost guaranteeing failure, especially for poor minority children. Hirsch's book didn't just argue this; it proved it conclusively, to my mind, offering an extraordinary *tour d'horizon* [a brief but comprehensive overview] of all the evidence about instructional methods that cognitive neuroscience had discovered.

If Hoxby and Peterson were right in asserting that markets were enough to fix our education woes, then the ed schools wouldn't be the disasters that Hirsch, Ravitch, and others have exposed. Unlike the government-run K–12 schools, the country's 1,500 ed schools represent an almost perfect system of choice, markets, and competition. Anyone interested in becoming a teacher is completely free to apply to any ed school that he or she wants. The ed schools, in turn, compete for students by offering competitive prices and—theoretically—attractive educational "products" (curricula and courses). Yet the schools are uniformly awful, the products the same dreary progressive claptrap. A few years ago, the National Council on Teacher Quality, a mainstream public education advocacy group, surveyed the nation's ed schools and found that almost all elementary education classes disdained phonics and scientific reading [that is, reading instruction based on research]. If the invisible hand is a surefire way to improve curriculum and instruction, as the incentivists insist, why does almost every teacher-in-training have to read the works of leftists Paolo Freire, Jonathan Kozol, and William Ayers—but usually nothing by, say, Hirsch or Ravitch?

For a good explanation, look to the concept of ideological hegemony, usually associated with the sociological Left. Instead of competition and diversity in the education schools, we confront what Hirsch calls the "thoughtworld" of teacher training, which operates like a Soviet-style regime suppressing alternative perspectives. Professors who dare to break with the ideological monopoly—who look to reading science or, say, embrace a core knowledge approach—won't get tenure, or get hired in the first place. The teachers they train thus wind up indoctrinated with the same pedagogical dogma whether they attend New York University's school of education or Humboldt State's [in California]. Those who put their faith in the power of markets to improve schools must at least show how their theory can account for the stubborn persistence of the thoughtworld.

Choice Will Not Work

Instead, we increasingly find the theory of educational competition detaching itself from its original school choice moorings and taking a new form. Vouchers may have stalled, but it's possible—or so many school reformers and education officials now assure us—to create the conditions for vigorous market competition *within* public school systems, with the same beneficent effects that were supposed to flow from a pure choice program.

Nowhere has this new philosophy of reform been more enthusiastically embraced than in the New York City school

Using Reading Research

After a century and a half of universal public education, and despite the highest per-pupil expenditure on elementary and secondary education in the world, 40 percent of U.S. fourth-graders can't read proficiently. That's according to the gold-standard NAEP (National Assessment of Educational Progress) tests. For minority students in inner-city schools, the reading failure rate is a catastrophic 65 percent. The consequences of this education failure are devastating. Children who don't read by fourth grade almost always fall behind in other subjects, often end up in costly special-education programs, and are more likely to drop out of school.

But this is an entirely self-inflicted wound. American scientists have figured out an answer to the reading-failure problem. For the past several decades, the National Institute of Child Health and Human Development . . . sponsored reading research by scientists in the field of cognitive neuroscience, pediatrics, and educational psychology. We now have hundreds of peer-reviewed studies that describe not just how children learn to read but also why so many fall behind, and how schools and teachers can keep this from happening.

But here's the scandal: in the education schools that train our future teachers, science is disdained. What's worse, education professors have convinced many school districts to choose reading programs for the classroom that satisfy the professor's philosophical beliefs about children but have no scientific support. When this happened in California in the 1980s, reading scores plummeted to the bottom in the nation.

"The Science of Reading Instruction and No Child Left Behind,"
Civic Bulletin, *September 2007. www.manhattan-institute.org.*

district under the control of Mayor Michael Bloomberg and schools chancellor Joel Klein. Gotham's schools are surging ahead with a host of market incentives, including models derived from the business world. Many of the country's major education foundations and philanthropies have boosted New York as the flagship school system for such market innovations, helping to spread the incentivist gospel nationally. Disciples of Klein have taken over the school systems in Baltimore and Washington, D.C., and Bloomberg's fellow billionaires Eli Broad and Bill Gates are about to launch a $60 million ad campaign to push the market approach during the presidential election season.

Don't get me wrong: market-style reforms are sometimes just what's necessary in the public schools. Over the past decade, for instance, I often called attention in *City Journal* to the destructively restrictive provisions in the New York City teachers' contract, which forced principals to hire teachers based solely on seniority, and I felt vindicated when negotiations between the Bloomberg administration and the United Federation of Teachers eliminated the seniority clause and created an open-market hiring system. Similarly, the teachers' lockstep salary schedule, based on seniority and accumulating useless additional education credits, is a counterproductive way to compensate the system's most important employees. The schools need a flexible salary structure that realistically reflects supply and demand in the teacher labor market.

Unfortunately, the Bloomberg administration and its supporters are pushing markets and competition in the public schools far beyond where the evidence leads. Everything in the system now has a price. Principals can get cash bonuses of as much as $50,000 by raising their schools' test scores; teachers in a few hundred schools now (and hundreds more later) can take home an extra $3,000 if the student scores in their schools improve; parents get money for showing up at parent-teacher conferences; their kids get money or—just what they need—cell phones for passing tests.

Much of this scaffolding of cash incentives (and career-ending penalties) rests on a rather shaky base: the state's highly unreliable reading and math tests in grades three through eight, plus the even more unreliable high school Regents exams [New York's statewide mandatory tests], which have been dumbed down so that schools will avoid federal sanctions under the No Child Left Behind act [a 2002 federal law that established national benchmarks for student achievement]. In the past, the tests have also been prone to cheating scandals. Expect more cheating as the stakes for success and failure rise.

While confidently putting their seal of approval on this market system, the mayor and chancellor appear to be agnostic on what actually works in the classroom. They've shown no interest, for example, in two decades' worth of scientific research sponsored by the National Institutes of Health that proves that teaching phonics and phonemic awareness is crucial to getting kids to read in the early grades. They have blithely retained a fuzzy math program, Everyday Math, despite a consensus of university math professors judging it inadequate. Indeed, Bloomberg and Klein have abjured all responsibility for curriculum and instruction and placed their bets entirely on choice, markets, and accountability.

But the new reliance on markets hasn't prevented special interests from hijacking the curriculum. One such interest is the Teachers College Reading and Writing Project—led by Lucy Calkins, the doyenne of the whole-language reading approach, which postulates that all children can learn to read and write naturally, with just some guidance from teachers, and that direct phonics instruction is a form of child abuse. Calkins's enterprise has more than $10 million in Department of Education contracts to guide reading and writing instruction in most of the city's elementary schools, even though no solid evidence supports her methodology. This may explain why, on the recent National Assessment of Educational Progress (NAEP) tests—widely regarded as a gold standard for educational assessment—Gotham students showed no improvement in fourth- and eighth-grade reading from 2003 to 2007, while the city of Atlanta, which hasn't staked everything on market incentives, has shown significant reading improvement.

One wonders why so many in the school reform movement and in the business community celebrate New York City's recent record on education. Is it merely because they hear the words "choice," "markets," and "competition" and think that all is well? If so, they're mistaken. The primal scene of all education reform is the classroom. If the teacher isn't doing the right thing, all the cash incentives in the world won't make a difference.

Success in Massachusetts

Those in the school reform movement seeking a case of truly spectacular academic improvement should look to Massachusetts, where something close to an education miracle has occurred. In the past several years, Massachusetts has improved more than almost every other state on the NAEP tests. In 2007, it scored first in the nation in fourth- and eighth-grade math and reading. The state's average scale scores on all four tests have also improved at far higher rates than most other states have seen over the past 15 years.

The improvement had nothing to do with market incentives. Massachusetts has no vouchers, no tuition tax credits, very few charter schools, and no market incentives for principals and teachers. The state owes its amazing improvement in student performance to a few key former education leaders, including state education board chairman John Silber, assistant commissioner Sandra Stotsky, and board member (and Manhattan Institute fellow) Abigail Thernstrom. Starting [in the late 1990s], these instructionists pushed the state's board of education to mandate a rigorous curriculum for all grades, created demanding tests linked to the curriculum standards, and insisted that all high school graduates pass a comprehensive exit exam. In its English Language Arts curriculum framework, the board even dared to say that reading instruction in the early grades should include systematic and explicit phonics. Now a professor of education reform at the University of Arkansas, Stotsky sums up: "The lesson from Massachusetts is that a strong content-based curriculum, together with upgraded certification regulations and teacher licensure tests that require teacher preparation programs to address that content, can be the best recipe for improving students' academic achievement."

The Massachusetts miracle doesn't prove that a standard curriculum and a focus on effective instruction will always produce academic progress. Nor does the flawed New York City experiment in competition mean that we should cast aside all market incentives in education. But what has transpired in these two places provides an important lesson: education reformers ought to resist unreflective support for elegant-sounding theories, derived from the study of economic activity, that don't produce verifiable results in the classroom. After all, children's lives are at stake.

> *"Charter schools . . . have graduation rates that far exceed state averages while serving a population more likely to be poor."*

Charter Schools Help Students

Tony Roberts

Tony Roberts is the chief executive officer of the Georgia Charter Schools Association, a nonprofit organization for charter school operators and petitioners. In the following viewpoint, he argues that local school districts that oppose the creation of charter schools are hurting students. Students who attend charter schools do better than those in public schools, and charter schools also improve the performance of public schools, he contends.

As you read, consider the following questions:

1. According to Roberts, what are charter schools, and what can they not do?

2. Article VIII, Section 1, Paragraph 1 of the Georgia state constitution, as cited by the author, says that what must be a primary obligation of the state of Georgia?

3. What is the composition of the student body of Ivy Preparatory Academy, according to Roberts?

Five school districts have filed suit against the state of Georgia claiming that the creation and operation of the Georgia Charter Schools Commission [which can approve new charter schools] is unconstitutional.

Additionally, they seek the closure of two charter schools[1] authorized by the commission: Ivy Preparatory Academy in Gwinnett County and Charter Conservatory for Liberal Arts and Technology [CCAT] in Bulloch County.

Lawsuits Unfounded

We believe that their suits are not only unfounded, but also a slap in the face to the parents and students who have decided to pursue the best public education possible.

First, we must understand what charter schools are. They are free, public, open enrollment schools that any student can attend. They cannot exclude students, they cannot charge tuition, and—like public schools everywhere—they must serve all students who wish to enroll in the school.

We also cannot forget that the commission was made necessary by local district denials of charter school applications. Prior to the creation of the commission, the approval rate for independent, public charter schools by local school districts was abysmal.

Local districts engaged in wholesale denials of charter school petitions with the weak rationale that the new schools would "not be in the best interests of the district." Districts had no incentive to give objective and fair consideration of proposed charter schools. And most did not. The commission merely creates a level playing field for charter approval.

---

1. Charter schools receive public money, but have different programs and accountability than most public schools. Students generally apply for or choose to attend them.

Comparison of Charter- and Public-School Test Scores in Gwinnett County, Georgia, 2009

This chart shows 2009 scores in reading on the Georgia statewide CRCT test for sixth graders at selected schools in Gwinnett County.

School	Percent of Students Who Met or Exceeded Reading Standards
Ivy Preparatory Academy (charter school)	93.7%
Trickum Middle	94.4%
Pinckneyville	94.0%
Richards Middle	87.1%
Creekland Middle	95.2%
Sweetwater Middle	85.7%
Five Forks Middle	97.8%
Shiloh Middle	91.0%

TAKEN FROM: Georgia Department of Education Web site, "CRCT— More 2009 Data," 2009. www.doe.kld.ga.us.

The districts might have stronger justification if there were not widespread problems with student achievement and graduation rates in traditional public schools.

While Georgia student achievement and graduation rates appear to be moving upward, there are still a lot of schools that do not serve their students well.

Let Students Out of Failing Schools

So, this issue really becomes, "shall we force children to continue attending schools that fail them?" The intent of the commission is to allow parents an option to seek a better education for their children in charter schools which, by the way, have graduation rates that far exceed state averages while serving a population more likely to be poor.

Ultimately, the lawsuit is about money. None of the districts had any problem when charter schools were authorized and funded at less than half the amount of funding compared to traditional public schools.

Only after the Legislature decided that charter schools should be funded equitably did they file suit.

But how does it make any sense for a district to retain state money for students it no longer teaches? The commission merely allows money to follow the child. Any opposite conclusion flies in the face of all notions of fairness and efficiency.

Districts further claim that the commission usurps their authority to control all public schools within their district and that this violates the Georgia Constitution.

Throughout the legislative process, numerous constitutional and legal experts reviewed the commission bill and deemed it fully constitutional. To be sure, the majority of our state legislators had no concerns about the bill's constitutionality when they passed it. Neither did Gov. Sonny Perdue when he signed it into law.

These plaintiff districts think the constitution gave them a monopoly on public education. Their fallacious argument is that the state has yielded total authority for public education over to the districts.

However, Article VIII, Section I, Paragraph 1 of the constitution makes the state's position very clear: "The provision of an adequate public education for the citizens shall be a primary obligation of the state of Georgia."

The citizens of Georgia want and deserve the best educational opportunities that their tax funds can provide. Ivy Preparatory Academy in Norcross and Charter Conservatory for Liberal Arts and Technology are shining examples of what can be accomplished in public education.

After its first year of operation, Ivy Prep has established itself as one of the top middle schools in the state.

This ethnically and socioeconomically diverse, all-girls school had more than 90 percent of its inaugural sixth-grade class meet or exceed CRCT [Criterion-Referenced Competency Tests, statewide Georgia assessment tests] standards in reading, English/language arts and math, a performance that rivaled or bested other public schools in the Gwinnett school district.

CCAT consistently graduates 100 percent of its students, outperforming both of the two traditional public high schools in Bulloch County and significantly higher than the state average.

Additionally, the number of students enrolling in college after graduation from CCAT is a full 20 percent higher than the state average.

It is no secret that charter schools in Georgia, especially independent public charter schools, outperform their peers in traditional public schools statewide. The opponents of charter schools claim that having charter schools harms the traditional public schools.

However, these opponents have not produced a single study that supports that claim. To the contrary, several university studies have concluded that the presence of quality charter schools increases the health and performance of traditional public schools.

There's a lot more riding on this suit than the settling of a theoretical constitutional question.

The most basic and most important question is: "What is best for the children?"

"Even though charter school students scored higher on standardized tests, the traditional public schools actually did a better job at raising test scores."

The Success of Charter Schools Is Exaggerated

Brian Jones

Brian Jones is a teacher, actor and activist in New York City. He has written for GritTV, SleptOn.com, and International Socialist Review. In the following viewpoint, he describes attending a party for parents at a charter school in New York City. Jones argues that the speakers at the party presented themselves as fighting on behalf of powerless minorities even though charter schools are supported by the powerful and provide little benefit to students. Jones concludes that parents, teachers, and unions must join together against the power elite to demand school improvements for all.

As you read, consider the following questions:

1. According to Jones, in comparison to charter schools, how many English language learners and special education students are served by traditional public schools?

Brian Jones, "The Charter School Charade," SocialistWorker.org, November 13, 2009. Reproduced by permission.

2. What are the Bradley Foundation and the Walton Family Foundation, according to the author?

3. Why does Jones believe that the speakers at the event he attended bring out the anti–charter school protests?

During the first week of October [2009], at faculty meetings across New York City, public school administrators warned their respective staff members to brace for a new round of budget cuts due at the end of [November 2009].

The very next day, Harlem Success Academy (HSA), a small but growing charter school[1] franchise, threw an open-bar back-to-school gala for parents and teachers at the Roseland Ballroom in midtown Manhattan.

The Appeal of Charter Schools

I attended this ball as the guest of a co-worker whose grandson attends one of the HSA schools (there are currently four in New York City). For more than a year now, I have written and spoken out against charter schools, but this trip gave me a new perspective on the debate; I'm glad I went.

As I entered the ballroom, one of several enthusiastic greeters welcomed me: "Don't forget to pick up your free drink tickets!" Orange balloons and streamers hung from every nook and cranny, a slideshow projected pictures of happy elementary schoolchildren in HSA uniforms, studying, playing chess, showing off artwork and so on. On the edge of the stage, a jazz band played, and just as I entered, the singer began belting out [soul and blues singer] Etta James' "At Last."

By the third time someone offered me hors d'oeuvres, I couldn't stop wondering: Who's paying for all of this?

My co-worker arrived and gave me an earful of what, from her perspective, makes HSA so great. "It's like a private

---

1. Charter schools receive public money, but have different programs and accountability than most public schools. Students generally apply for or choose to attend charter schools.

school," she told me. "My grandson is learning the same thing the kids downtown are learning. He loves to go to school."

Besides what she sees as a stronger curriculum (including foreign language study in elementary school), my co-worker returned again and again to the issue of student and parent behavior. "They don't tolerate what we tolerate," she said several times. What is it HSA doesn't tolerate? According to my co-worker: disruptive children and parents who don't play an active role in their child's education.

I asked her to elaborate on this difference between the public school where she and I work, and the HSA school her grandson attends. What does it mean to "not tolerate" disruptive children or non-attentive parents? It means, essentially, that you and your child can be removed from the school for failure to comply with your HSA contract. For parents, that means not only signing your child's homework every night, but your presence at your child's HSA soccer game is mandatory! "It's like they're teaching you how to be a parent," my co-worker told me.

Given the scale of the [2009 economic] crisis (Black unemployment is rising four times faster than white unemployment in New York City), it's not surprising to hear that parents are eager to rescue their kids from the devastation other families are experiencing. "But what about parents who work two jobs?" I asked, "What about parents who can't do all of that?" My co-worker didn't have an answer.

Protests Against Charter Schools

As the ballroom began to fill up with hundreds of Black and Latino parents, I began to notice young teachers arriving in groups, many wearing large buttons that said, "Hi-five me, I'm a teacher!" Standing in the back of the Roseland ballroom, it sure seemed like everyone—kids, teachers and parents—was happy. As the old saying goes, it's hard to argue with success.

Then the program began.

First, we were shown a video that told the story of Harlem Success Academy. The camera dropped in on teachers working in colorful, clean classrooms. We saw children at work and at play. Everyone was smiling and laughing.

In one segment, children took turns dancing for a worm's-eye-view camera, finishing each set of moves by flashing a piece of paper with a large "4" at the lens—which was meant to indicate a top score on one of New York state's standardized tests. The music for this celebration of test scores was upbeat and irresistible. I found myself feeling sorry for a boy who did his best for the camera, but only had a "3" to hold up.

To my surprise, the next segment featured many of the protests against charter schools that have taken place around the city. At one point, they showed the picket line from the very first day of school at PS [Public School] 123. The line formed at the separate HSA entrance to the building.

"Can you believe that? They protested at a *school!*" my coworker fumed, her voice full of disgust. I responded, "What they're *not* showing you is what HSA did to PS 123. They took over more classrooms and dumped the teachers' stuff into PS 123 classrooms—*that's* why they're protesting."

Those demonstrations, to my surprise, turned out to be a theme of the night. Again and again, we heard about the "protesters outside." The very first speaker was an HSA parent. "There are protesters outside here tonight," she told the crowd. "We want to let them know that they can't push us aside!"

Next up was the CEO of Harlem Success Academy, Eva Moskowitz. She went for her biggest applause line early in her remarks. Bragging about HSA's high test scores last year [2008], she pumped her fist in the air: "We didn't just meet Scarsdale [a wealthy New York suburb], we BEAT Scarsdale!"

First of all, show me a teacher who doesn't think that last year's test scores were grossly inflated to boost [New York

City] Mayor Michael Bloomberg's re-election bid, and I'll show you a teacher who doesn't work in New York City.

Enrolling High Scorers

But even taking those scores at face value, it turns out that the secret to HSA's success has less to do with improving scores than with enrolling high scorers.

A recent NYC Department of Education accountability report—released to the public, but very quietly—shows that traditional public schools serve more than three times more English Language Learners and nearly twice as many Special Education students as charter schools. But according to the same report, even though charter school students scored higher on standardized tests, the traditional public schools actually did a better job at raising test scores.

To be honest, I couldn't hear much of what Moskowitz had to say. After a few initial cheers, parents and teachers became more interested in talking to each other, and simply drowned her out. At one point, she spent several minutes shushing the audience.

From what I did hear, her most revealing remarks came at the very end, when she introduced New York City schools Chancellor Joel Klein. "If you're the U.S. Postal Service, you don't exactly embrace FedEx," she told us, "but this chancellor has done that."

It took me a moment to pick my jaw up off the floor. Moskowitz's metaphor spoke volumes about the charter school "movement." For parents, of course, it's about trying to find something better for their kids. For Moskowitz, it's about privatization and union-busting—FedEx has not only fought off every attempt to unionize delivery drivers, it doesn't even call them employees! The drivers are classified as "independent contractors," which makes them ineligible for (among other things) unemployment benefits. Is that her vision for the way teachers should be treated?

For his part, Klein didn't seem the slightest bit embarrassed at the comparison. He was beaming as he rose to the podium. "I'm thrilled to be among you," he began. "You don't tolerate mediocrity. You insist on excellence!"

Over the din of hundreds of casual conversations, Klein, too, was mostly inaudible. I could make out the themes, though. He mostly talked about the civil rights movement. He mentioned that his wife had clerked for [African American Supreme Court justice] Thurgood Marshall. Describing the education system of those days, he concluded: "It sure was separate, but it was never equal."

He went on to praise Harlem Success Academy for finally fulfilling the mission of the civil rights movement. I thought to myself: Surely, he realizes he's speaking to an audience entirely composed of Black and Latino parents! Surely, he realizes that he's speaking to people who *still* attend segregated schools! What was the point of his message? That HSA schools "may be separate, but *now* they're equal"?

Who needs *Brown v. Board of Education*? Klein seemed pleased to have fulfilled the promise of *Plessey v. Ferguson*![2] I have a hard time believing this irony would have been lost on Thurgood Marshall himself.

The Elite Support Charter Schools

Just when I was ready to make my exit, the next speaker caught my attention. He was a tall, African American man. By his age, and dynamic manner of speaking, I supposed he was a veteran activist. Clearly, this man was on the side of charter schools, though, so I was interested to hear what he had to say. "That's Dr. Fuller," my co-worker told me.

Dr. Howard Fuller, I would later learn, was a Black Power activist who became a privatization-obsessed insider long ago. As Klein has in New York, Fuller spent his four years as super-

2. *Plessy v. Ferguson* was an 1896 Supreme Court case that upheld racial segregation. It was repudiated in 1954 by *Brown v. Board of Education*, which desegregated schools.

Charter Schools Not Always Better

The group portrait [of charter schools] shows wide variation in performance. A study [by the Center for Research on Education Outcomes] reveals that a decent fraction of charter schools, 17 percent, provide superior education opportunities for their students. Nearly half of the charter schools nationwide have results that are no different from the local public school options and over a third, 37 percent, deliver learning results that are significantly worse than their student would have realized had they remained in traditional public schools. These findings underlie the parallel findings of significant state-by-state differences in charter school performance and in the national aggregate performance of charter schools. The policy challenge is how to deal constructively with varying levels of performance today and into the future.

CREDO,
Multiple Choice: Charter School Performance in 16 States,
2009. http://credo.stanford.edu.

intendent of Milwaukee's public schools pushing privatization. He was an early proponent of school vouchers and later served as an education adviser to [U.S. president] George W. Bush. His mission in life seems to be lending "civil rights" credentials (and thus African American support) to privatization schemes.

The organization he founded, the Black Alliance for Educational Options was made possible by the generosity of the Bradley Foundation and Walton Family Foundation. The Bradley Foundation is infamous for sponsoring the activities of racists such as David Horowitz (who authored the "Ten Reasons Reparations for Slavery Is a Bad Idea—and Racist, Too" ad) and Charles Murray (whose book *The Bell Curve* argued that African Americans were intellectually inferior). The Walton Family, of course, owns Wal-Mart and is one of the top donors to right-wing causes (such as opposing affirmative action) nationwide.

As I listened to Fuller's speech, I knew none of this. But in retrospect, his credentials shed light on his remarks—particularly the way he began. "I'm not going to ask you to be quiet," he thundered, "I'm going to talk right over you!"

He poured out contempt for the anti-charter school protesters. "Why would anyone protest you sending your kids to a great school?" he asked, his voice thick with sarcasm. Of course, he made no mention of the boxes, books and furniture that HSA piled up in PS 123 classrooms this summer or the overcrowding caused by HSA's "natural" growth.

All of this was just the warm-up, though. Fuller's main act was to channel [nineteen-century African American antislavery activist] Frederick Douglass.

Judging by the noise, almost no one was listening as Fuller raised himself to his full height and conjured from memory a lengthy selection from the great abolitionist's famous argument that "if there is no struggle, there is no progress!" He boomed, "Power concedes nothing without a demand. It never has, and it never will."

I don't know about you, but when I think of people with "power," I think of [U.S. president] Barack Obama or Michael Bloomberg or even Joel Klein. Each of those figures is a staunch advocate for charter schools. So what "struggle" could Fuller possibly be talking about? And as for the "power" he wants to see concede, I can only think that he must be referring to the United Federation of Teachers [a major teachers' union].

With that thought, the whole evening clicked together for me like the pieces of a puzzle. *That's* why the video and the speakers made such a big deal out of the anti-charter school protests—the whole point is for the charter school "activists," who have nothing *but* power (not to mention money) at their backs, to paint *themselves* as underdogs.

Parents Against Teachers

But I learned something else from attending this event. My co-worker and her grandson are genuinely happy with Harlem Success Academy. Those of us who think it's important to defend public education have to find a way to talk to people like her, or we're sunk.

In 1968, my union went on strike *against* the aspirations of a section of the Black community to have control over their own schools. Since that time, it's been all too easy for city administrators to pit parents against teachers. Parents—especially African American parents—have seen their kids' educational opportunities shrivel, and teachers have conceded away precious rights in contract after contract. Here, another Frederick Douglass quotation actually does fit: "They divided both to conquer each."

My union better hurry up and figure out how to overcome this division, or pretty soon, there won't be much of a union left.

Nowhere is this truer than in Harlem. The public elementary school where I work in East Harlem has lost 30 students to charter schools since September [2009]. It's time that teachers use whatever muscle we have left to wage a serious fight to make the public schools a place kids will love to attend. Parents should be our natural allies in this struggle.

The first step is recognizing that public education will only be fixed not by destroying it nor by funneling public money to private entities, but by giving *every* school the kind of resources we know are needed to make *great* schools.

The second step is remembering that power concedes nothing without a demand. It never has, and it never will.

Periodical Bibliography

The following articles have been selected to supplement the diverse views presented in this chapter.

Nick Anderson	"Study: Charter School Growth Accompanied by Racial Imbalance," *Washington Post*, February 4, 2010.
Clint Bolick and Laura Underkuffler	"Are School Vouchers the Next Great Civil Rights Issue?" *Legal Affairs*, June 13, 2005.
Martin Carnoy, Frank Adamson, Amita Chudgar	"Vouchers and Public School Performance: A Case Study of the Milwaukee Parental Choice Program," Economic Policy Institute, October 2, 2007. www.epi.org.
George A. Clowes	"Can Vouchers Reform Public Schools?" Heartland Institute, 2008. www.heartland.org.
Arne Duncan	"School Reform Means Doing What's Best for Kids," *Wall Street Journal*, April 22, 2009.
Education Week	"Vouchers," December 6, 2007. www.edweek.org.
Clara Hemphill	"Do Charter Schools Help or Hurt?" *Huffington Post*, July 15, 2009. www.huffingtonpost.com.
National Education Association	"The Case Against Vouchers," n.d. www.nea.org.
Greg Toppo	"More Black Lawmakers Open to School Vouchers," *USA Today*, May 12, 2009.
Wall Street Journal	"No Child Left Behind," November 4, 2009.
Marcus A. Winters	"Charters' Promise," *City Journal*, September 28, 2009.

For Further Discussion

Chapter 1

1. Linda Darling-Hammond says that the problem with No Child Left Behind (NCLB) is that it incorrectly assumes that "what schools need is more carrots and sticks rather than fundamental changes." Would Pete Wright agree that NCLB is too focused on "carrots and sticks," or does he seem to think that carrots and sticks are helpful? Explain your answer.

2. Bruno Behrend argues that Illinois can reduce taxes and yet improve its schools. Which do you think is more important to him: the lower taxes or the better schools? Do you think the changes proposed by the Center for Tax and Budget Accountability would require an increase in taxes, and does that seem like a fair trade-off?

3. The Center for Union Facts argues that teachers' unions in Washington, D.C., acted unreasonably in 1992 when they protested the elimination of a preparation period by refusing to write college recommendations. Do you agree that the teachers' union acted unreasonably? If teachers feel they are treated unfairly, or that school policies will hurt their ability to teach, what do you think they should do?

Chapter 2

1. Would you rather be evaluated through the kinds of Danish tests Bill Ferriter discusses, or would you rather be evaluated through the multiple choice tests Patrick Mattimore advocates? Which tests do you think would be fairer? Which do you think would give teachers a better sense of your progress? Explain your answers.

2. Monty Neill argues that standardized high school graduation tests are used disproportionately in states with
   Spanish-speaking students. Paul Greenberg argues that it
   is especially important to make sure Spanish-speaking
   students master English. Do you think that Spanish-
   speaking students *should* be required to prove mastery of
   English before they graduate from high school? Would
   such a requirement aimed especially at Spanish-speaking
   students be discriminatory, as Neill suggests, or would it
   show a commitment to integrating them into American
   culture, as Greenberg suggests? Explain your answers.

Chapter 3

1. David B. Cohen and Alex Kajitani argue that test scores
   are a poor measure of student achievement and take time
   away from teaching important concepts. Camille Esch suggests that this problem could be addressed by developing
   new tests. Do you think new tests would address Cohen
   and Kajitani's concerns? Why or why not?

2. Maisie McAdoo claims that Andy Smarick "doesn't say
   what should happen" with the students in public schools
   that are shut down. Is this true? What does Smarick seem
   to believe will happen with students who leave failing
   schools? Based on your reading of McAdoo's and
   Smarick's viewpoints, do you think students who leave a
   failing school would be better off or worse off? Explain
   your answer.

Chapter 4

1. Greg Forster argues that Americans should think about
   education the way they think about other goods and services, like "food, housing, clothing, transportation, or
   medical care." Are any of these goods and services subsi-
   dized by the government? Does the government have a
   duty to provide food, housing, clothing, transportation

and medical care to all, the way that it is often considered to have a duty to provide schooling to all? What consequences does this have for using choice for schooling, if any?

2. Both Tony Roberts and Brian Jones discuss the issue of state funds being taken away from regular public schools and given to charter schools, which enroll some of the public schools' former students. Based on Roberts's and Jones's discussion, do you think it is fair to take money from public schools in order to give it to charter schools in these situations? Why or why not?

Organizations to Contact

American Federation of Teachers (AFT)

555 New Jersey Ave. NW, Washington, DC 20001

(202) 879-4400

Web site: www.aft.org

The AFT is an American labor union that represents teachers, paraprofessionals, and school-related personnel; local, state, and federal employees; higher education faculty and staff; and nurses and other health-care professionals and is affiliated with the umbrella union organization the AFL-CIO. It has more than three thousand local affiliates nationwide and more than 1.3 million members. Its Web site includes news, reports, and press releases. Its periodicals include *American Teacher, American Educator, AFT On Campus, PSRP Reporter, Health-wire,* and *Public Employee Advocate.*

Bill and Melinda Gates Foundation

PO Box 23350, Seattle, WA 98102

(206) 709-3100

e-mail: info@gatesfoundation.org

Web site: www.gatesfoundation.org

The Gates Foundation is the largest transparently operated private foundation in the world. Among its primary goals are the expansion of educational opportunities and access to information technology in the United States through the use of grants and philanthropic giving. The Gates Foundation United States Program Web page includes numerous resources on education, including research reports, standards, fact sheets, commentary, speeches, and many other materials related to the foundation's strategies and educational programs.

The Carnegie Foundation for the Advancement of Teaching

51 Vista Lane, Stanford, CA   94305
(650) 566-5100 • fax: (650) 326-0278
Web site: www.carnegiefoundation.org

The Carnegie Foundation is an independent policy and research center that specializes in teaching. Its program areas include K–12, undergraduate, and graduate and professional education. Its Web site includes articles and resources, and it publishes numerous books and pamphlets, such as *Organizing Schools for Improvement: Lessons from Chicago.*

Center for American Progress

1333 H Street NW, 10th floor, Washington, DC   20005
(202) 682-1611
e-mail: progress@americanprogress.org
Web site: www.americanprogress.org

The Center for American Progress is a progressive think tank with an interest in values like diversity, shared and personal responsibility, and participatory government. Its Web site includes articles and reports such as "Leaders and Laggards: A State-by-State Report Card on Educational Innovation," and "Stimulating Excellence: Unleashing the Power of Innovation in Education."

FairTest: National Center for Fair and Open Testing

342 Broadway, Cambridge, MA   02139
(617) 864-4810 • fax: (617) 497-2224
Web site: www.fairtest.org

FairTest is an organization that advocates for the reform of current standardized testing and assessment practices in education and employment. It publishes a regular electronic newsletter, the *Examiner*, plus a full catalog of materials on both K–12 and university testing to aid teachers, administrators, students, parents, and researchers.

The Heritage Foundation

214 Massachusetts Ave. NE, Washington, DC   20002
(202) 546-4400 • fax: (202) 546-8328
e-mail: info@heritage.org
Web site: www.heritage.org

The Heritage Foundation is a conservative public policy re-search institute dedicated to the principles of free and com-petitive enterprise, limited government, and individual liberty. In education, it devotes particular attention to promoting school choice. Its Web site includes reports such as "More Government Preschool: An Expensive and Unnecessary Middle-Class Subsidy" and "School Choice in Sweden."

National Alliance for Public Charter Schools

1101 Fifteenth Street NW, Suite 1010, Washington, DC   20005
(202) 289-2700 • fax: (202) 289-4009
Web site: www.publiccharters.org

The National Alliance for Public Charter Schools is a national nonprofit organization committed to advancing the charter school movement through education and advocacy. Its Web site includes press releases, issue pages, and downloadable publications such as "How State Charter Laws Rank Against the New Model Public School Law," and "Alliance Comments on Investing in Innovation (i3) Proposed Priorities, Require-ments, Definitions, and Selection Criteria."

National Association of Elementary School Principals (NAESP)

1615 Duke Street, Alexandria, VA   22314
(800) 386-2377 • fax: (800) 396-2377
e-mail: naesp@naesp.org
Web site: www.naesp.org

NAESP provides support for elementary and middle school principals and administrators. It offers reports and research on many issues, including measuring academic performance and the debates over charter schools. Among the publications it distributes are *Principal Magazine,* the monthly newsletter *Communicator,* the bimonthly e-newsletter *Before the Bell,* and the quarterly e-newsletter *Research Roundup.*

National Education Association (NEA)

1201 Sixteenth Street NW, Washington, DC   20036
(202) 883-8400 • fax: (202) 822-7974
Web site: www.nea.org

The NEA is the largest union in the United States, representing public school teachers and support personnel, faculty and staffers at colleges and universities, retired educators, and college students preparing to become teachers. Two of NEA's many publications are the monthly magazine *NEA Today Online* and the biannual report *Thoughts and Action.*

U.S. Department of Education

400 Maryland Ave. SW, Washington, DC   20202
(800) USA-LEARN (872-5327)
Web site: www.ed.gov

The Department of Education is the cabinet level department of the U.S. government responsible for overseeing education. Its Web site includes reports and research, such as "Effects of Preschool Curriculum Programs on School Readiness" and "Evaluation of the D.C. Opportunity Scholarship Program: Impacts After Three Years."

Bibliography of Books

Scott Abernathy — *No Child Left Behind and the Public Schools*. Ann Arbor: University of Michigan Press, 2007.

Martin Carnoy, Rebecca Jacobsen, Lawrence Mishel, and Richard Rothstein — *The Charter School Dust-Up: Examining the Evidence on Enrollment and Achievement*. New York: Teachers College Press and Economic Policy Institute, 2005.

Mary Compton and Lois Weiner — *The Assault on Teaching, Teachers, and Their Unions: Stories for Resistance*. New York: Palgrave Macmillan, 2008.

Leigh Dingerson, Barbara Miner, Bob Peterson, and Stephanie Walters — *Keeping the Promise? The Debate over Charter Schools*. Milwaukee: Rethinking Schools, 2008.

Emily Van Dunk and Anneliese M. Dickman — *School Choice and the Question of Accountability: The Milwaukee Experience*. Ann Arbor, MI: Sheridan Books, 2003.

Patricia Gandara and Frances Contreras — *The Latino Education Crisis: The Consequences of Failed Social Policies*. Cambridge, MA: Harvard University Press, 2009.

Ofelia Garcia — *Bilingual Education in the 21st Century: A Global Perspective*. Malden, MA: John Wiley, 2009.

William Hayes   *No Child Left Behind*. Lanham, MD: Rowman and Littlefield Education, 2008.

Frederick M. Hess   *Common Sense School Reform*. New York: Palgrave Macmillan, 2004.

William G. Howell and Paul E. Peterson   *The Education Gap: Vouchers and Urban Schools*. Rev. ed. Washington, DC: Brookings Institution Press, 2006.

Daniel Koretz   *Measuring Up: What Educational Testing Really Tells Us*. Cambridge, MA: Harvard University Press, 2008.

Jay Mathews   *Work Hard, Be Nice: How Two Inspired Teachers Created the Most Promising Schools in America*. Chapel Hill, NC: Algonquin Books, 2009.

Patrick J. McGuinn   *No Child Left Behind and the Transformation of Federal Education Policy, 1965–2005*. Lawrence: University Press of Kansas, 2006.

Terry M. Moe   *Schools, Vouchers, and the American Public*. Washington, DC: Brookings Institution Press, 2002.

Joseph F. Murphy and Coby V. Meyers   *Turning Around Failing Schools: Leadership Lessons from the Organizational Sciences*. Thousand Oaks, CA: Corwin, 2007.

Nel Noddings   *When School Reform Goes Wrong*. New York: Teachers College Press, 2007.

Rod Paige   *The War Against Hope: How Teachers'*
                     Unions Hurt Children, Hinder
                     Teachers, and Endanger Public
                     Education. Nashville: Thomas Nelson,
                     2009.

Linda Perlstein   *Tested: One American School Struggles*
                     to Make the Grade. New York: Henry
                     Holt, 2007.

Richard Phelps   *Kill the Messenger: The War on*
                     Standardized Testing. Edison, NJ:
                     Transaction, 2005.

Diane Ravitch   *The Death and Life of the Great*
                     American School System: How Testing
                     and Choice Are Undermining
                     Education. New York: Basic Books,
                     2010.

Mary Lee Smith   *Political Spectacle.* New York:
et al.   Routledge, 2004.

Brian M. Stetcher   *Pain and Gain: Implementing No*
                     Child Left Behind in Three States,
                     2004–2006. Santa Monica, CA: Rand,
                     2008.

Herbert J.   *School Choice: The Findings.*
Walberg   Washington, DC: Cato Institute,
                     2007.

Index